IT'S JUST A THOUGHT

*A collection of ideas about
God in everyday life*

Doreen Warman

To
David and my family

© 1997 Trustees for Methodist Church Purposes
Published by Foundery Press

Cover designed by Steven Hall

ISBN 1 85852 086 X

FOREWORD

Where do we look for God? Some people go to church, others into the countryside where they can feel close to the beauty of nature. Yet wherever we go there is often a feeling that we have to be in a special place before we are in the presence of the one who has created us. We often envy those who seem to 'walk with God' in the ordinariness of their everyday lives and wonder how we can begin to discover God's presence when we are washing up at the kitchen sink or standing in the rain waiting for the bus which was due ten minutes age.

Doreen Warman has the ability to find God in the most mundane places and with a gentle blend of insight and humour she invites us to view situations through her eyes. Here is someone who discovers God in the humdrum of the ordinary.

I am sure *It's Just A Thought* will find its way on to coffee tables and bedside cabinets, into briefcases and desks, to be read on buses and trains, in sitting rooms, bedrooms and in hospital wards. It will become a treasured possession which will be read and re-read. This is the kind of book you can open on any page and find something to set you thinking. My hope is that it will also be used in house groups to stimulate discussion and as each 'thought' is accompanied by a scripture reading and a prayer it also provides a choice of epilogues for any meeting.

What a joy it is to write an introduction to this collection of 'thoughts' – I do hope you will enjoy reading them as much as I have.

Revd Sandy Williams, MEd, MA
November 1997

CONTENTS

New Year

Spring/Easter

Pentecost

Summer

Harvest/Autumn

Christmas

Winter/End of Year

1

Thank God

'It's a beautiful morning, thank God.' So said the smiling young woman who served breakfast in an Irish guest house. What a joyous sentiment to start the day!

If we are honest we will probably admit that our usual reasons for thanking God are rather more self-interested. We thank him for seeing us through the big crises of our lives – for recovery from illness, for passing our exams, for deliverance from danger, and safe returns.

It's only when things go wrong that we seem to appreciate the way they were before. It's only when we recover from lumbago that we give thanks for being able to bend down!

We thank God when the storm is over, and when the harvest is brought in, and then we go on our way, grumbling at the change in the weather and the price of bread! And yet the miracles of life are all around us every day. We turn on the tap and there is water; we flick on a switch and there is light. We wake up in the morning and there we are – breathing – and living – and thinking (well, some of the time!). Thank God!

Thanking God can become a way of life. Once we are truly conscious of thanksgiving in the little things of every day, we become more aware of his presence all around us. Instead of just 'thanking God' we begin 'thinking God', and our lives take on a new dimension.

It's just a thought . . .

READING

Psalm 136:1-4

O give thanks to the LORD, for he is good,
    for his steadfast love endures forever.
O give thanks to the God of gods,
    for his steadfast love endures forever.
O give thanks to the Lord of lords,
    for his steadfast love endures forever;
who alone does great wonders,
    for his steadfast love endures forever.

PRAYER

Generous God, your love enfolds our lives. Like children in a comfortable home we take your parenting for granted. Open our eyes to appreciate your gifts. Open our hearts to feel your care. Open our hands to share your goodness with others. Amen.

2

How do you do?

'What are you dooning, Nanny?' inquired my two-year-old grandson following me from room to room on a recent visit – a question which has since become a family byword! 'I'm just peeling these apples', or (more excitingly) 'trying to unblock the sink' were among the replies. Not exactly earth-shaking activities by any standard.

It's probably only when someone asks the question that we stop to consider what we *are* doing with our lives! We cannot all be involved in great and heroic feats – surgeons performing lifesaving operations, or climbers scaling Everest. The mundane routine of living may seem a very small contribution to society's well-being.

Looking at the nations of the world we may well ask, 'What are they doing?' Are they building, learning, growing together? Or – as we see on the TV news – tearing one another apart in vendettas of hatred and greed? 'What can we do about it?' we ask, and the answer seems to be 'very little'. Maybe we collect for Christian Aid, or give support to a petition, donate our discarded clothes to a charity shop or increase our weekly offering. Perhaps the most significant way we can work for harmony in the world is by making sure that our own relationships are free from bitterness and strife and that we show tolerance and understanding in our everyday dealings with one another.

In one of her rare TV interviews, Mother Teresa explained how those whom her community had helped had gone on to help others and so had radiated God's love across the globe. When faced with a seemingly impossible task she said, 'It's not how much we do but how much love we put into it.'

It's just a thought . . .

READING

1 Peter 4:8-11

Above all, maintain constant love for one another, for love covers a multitude of sins. Be hospitable to one another without complaining. Like good stewards of the manifold grace of God, serve one another with whatever gift each of you has received. Whoever speaks must do so as one speaking the very words of God; whoever serves must do so with the strength that God supplies, so that God may be glorified in all things through Jesus Christ.

PRAYER

God of love, show us how to serve you in ordinary ways. In our search for your kingdom help us to look not only at the wider world but also close to home. Remind us that if we would follow you we need to show your love to everyone we meet, in every task we undertake, and on every day of our lives.

3

Handle with care

I had a fight today! Not a mental struggle, or a mere battle of words, but a real physical, hand-to-hand *fight!* A shocking admission, I know, and although I emerged victorious, suffering from nervous exhaustion and a torn fingernail, it was small consolation to see my opponent lying crushed and broken at my feet.

I am not normally given to violence, but when I explain that my victim was a packet of biscuits, you will no doubt sympathise, especially as I had already had a bout of three rounds with a pork pie wrapped in cellophane, and a long and painful contest with a tin of corned beef!

I have tried reading the instructions on packaged food, but 'Pierce with a pin and push off' or 'Insert coin and twist' simply do not work for me and I always read 'Open other end' too late! There is so much 'sealed-in freshness', 'boil-in-the-bag goodness' and 'untouched by hand' hygiene today that the package must often cost more than the contents.

Does the same thing apply to our Christianity? Have we wrapped it, sealed it and packaged it to such an extent that people find it difficult to discover the 'truth' within? Do we sometimes make the Christian life unnecessarily complicated? The parables of Jesus were simple, directly concerned with everyday life, and of his work we read that 'he went about doing good'.

The danger is that as we become more and more organised, so committees, meetings and intellectual discussions may take the place of those spontaneous acts of neighbourliness which give life to our faith – the friendly visit, the thoughtful letter or helping hand. An Annual Report is a poor substitute for these!

It's just a thought . . .

READING

Luke 10:25-28

Just then a lawyer stood up to test Jesus. 'Teacher,' he said, 'what must I do to inherit eternal life?' He said to him, 'What is written in the law? What do you read there?' He answered, 'You shall love the Lord your God with all your heart, and with all your soul, and with all your strength, and with all your mind; and your neighbour as yourself.' And he said to him, 'You have given the right answer; do this, and you will live.'

PRAYER

We thank you, God, that you have revealed your purposes not only to the learned and wise, but to all your children who trust you. Help us to accept your law of love in all its directness and not to obscure your message with hindrances of our own making.

4

Make do or mend?

'It just came to bits in my hand!' That was the day when the door handle of my car broke off and complicated manoeuvres were required to extricate the passengers!

It was also the day when the knife slipped as I was chopping carrots for the evening meal. It requires some acrobatic skill to open the First Aid box and unwrap a plaster with one hand, whilst holding the other under the cold tap!

Elaborate operations with super-glue, bolts and metal strips reinforced and repaired the handle which, alas, has since disintegrated again.

I was more successful with the cut finger. After a few applications of antiseptic cream it healed up as good as new!

What a remarkable thought! A cut finger, or a grazed knee, or even a broken bone will mend in time, but no matter how we glue and screw, manufactured materials can only be repaired, not healed!

Perhaps it is this wonderful capacity to grow together again which most distinguishes us from our furniture – the living world of the Creator from our machine-made world.

It is surely the same with more spiritual matters. Broken relationships between people or nations can sometimes be patched up by human ingenuity. We can build bridges and pass laws, we can redevelop and reconstruct the ruins, but it is only when there is a God-given spirit of reconciliation at work that the deep-seated rifts between the peoples of our world will be truly healed.

It's just a thought . . .

READING

2 Corinthians 5:17-19

So if anyone is in Christ, there is a new creation: everything old has passed away; see, everything has become new! All this is from God, who reconciled us to himself through Christ, and has given us the ministry of reconciliation; that is, in Christ God was reconciling the world to himself, not counting their trespasses against them, and entrusting the message of reconciliation to us.

PRAYER

Jesus, the great physician, touch our lives. Pour the balm of your love on our wounded world. Mend our broken relationships by the power of your Holy Spirit so that we may grow together again and be healed.

5

Call in the experts

It was one of those weeks! . . . The Plumber arrived to put a new
tank in the loft on the very morning that the Piano Tuner came to
tune the piano – our dog had an appointment at the Poodle
Parlour, and my youngest daughter developed the beginnings of
an abscess on her tooth! My husband had removed the back door
for repair and (after weeks of drought) it began to pour with rain!

As I listened to the strident bashing of pipes in the airing
cupboard, combined with the discordant strumming of the piano, I
began to wonder what the Dog Beautician would have done about
the swollen tooth, how the Plumber would have trimmed the dog,
and whether the Dentist would be able to 'scale' the piano or fill
the hole in our back door!

As it was, the Tuner tuned, the Plumber plumbed, the dog was
expertly trimmed, the Dentist saved the tooth, and – yes – the
back door was put back on its hinges.

There are some jobs that are best done by the Experts! We do not
hesitate to send for the Doctor when we have a pain but, strangely,
we are far more reluctant to send for an Expert when we are sad,
or cross or worried! Instead we try to escape – we call in the
Entertainers, the Politicians, the Accountants, the Psychiatrists –
but there is only one Expert who has experience of all life's
problems and difficulties. We meet him in many different ways,
including the loving understanding of others, the wonder of his
world and the beauty of music. God is on call day and night – get
in touch with him and he will give us immediate attention. There
will not even be a bill – for his services are free to all!

It's just a thought . . .

READING

2 Samuel 22:31-33

This God – his way is perfect;
     the promise of the LORD proves true;
     he is a shield for all who take refuge in him.
For who is God, but the LORD?
     And who is a rock, except our God?
The God who has girded me with strength
     has opened wide my path.

PRAYER

God, who loves us, you know what we need before we ask. You are more than willing to help us. Forgive us because we do not turn to you often enough. Forgive us because we try to solve our problems on our own. Forgive us because we are too proud to admit that we need your help and because we do not trust you enough to provide for us.

6

Treasure in heaven

It seemed such a good idea to install a loft ladder and take some of the strain out of those trips to the attic world. 'Fitted in minutes' was the legend on the side of the box, a somewhat optimistic estimate as it turned out!

First item on the agenda was to clear a space in the loft for storing the ladder – a week's work in itself. And what treasures we discovered! Boxes of old snapshots, two battered hockey sticks, one fish tank (slightly cracked), four dozen empty jam jars, one stringless violin, two suspect electric fires, one carpet underlay . . . and much, much more! Things we had been reluctant to throw away – they might come in handy one day!

On a visit to Covent Garden I spent an interesting hour looking round the 'Antique' stalls. From teaspoons to telescopes, fish forks to fire irons, I was amazed at what I saw. Plates and jugs in Thirties style which I remembered as everyday objects from my childhood suddenly appeared as collector's items! We cannot all expect to discover a Rembrandt under the rafters, but how many of us could have foreseen that Granny's bannister brush would become a museum piece? Perhaps we would all like to be the person on the *Antiques Roadshow* whose possession turns out to be valuable. How do we know what to keep and what to throw away? One person's rubbish is another person's treasure!

One thing is certain – we cannot take it with us (thank goodness).

So let us store not up for ourselves treasure in the loft where moth and dust doth corrupt, but rather treasure in heaven – moments of laughter, words of wisdom, whatsoever is pure and lovely and of good report – for these will not tarnish and decay, they take up very little room and their value can only increase!

It's just a thought . . .

READING

Luke 12:32-34

Do not be afraid, little flock, for it is your Father's good pleasure to give you the kingdom. Sell your possessions, and give alms. Make purses for yourselves that do not wear out, an unfailing treasure in heaven, where no thief comes near and no moth destroys. For where your treasure is, there your heart will be also.

PRAYER

Lord God, the auditor of our accounts, we live in a society dominated by the profit motive, where success is measured by material possessions and social standing. We have forgotten how to discriminate between short-term gain and lasting enrichment. Be our appraiser. Help us to recognise what is of value in your sight and to set our hearts on worthwhile treasure.

7

Sandwiches

Back to school, back to work, back to routine, and there I was making sandwiches again. I sometimes thought I could make sandwiches in my sleep! If I made twelve rounds of sandwiches five days per week for twenty years that would be one hundred and twenty-four thousand eight hundred slices of bread. It could be a record!

My interest in sandwiches began, I think, during the war, when, as an evacuee, I took a packed lunch to school every day. It was always raining in those days, I was always homesick, and the sandwiches were always *paste*.

I am happy to say that my repertoire has widened since to include such exotic varieties as Danish Open Sandwiches, Toasted Sandwiches and even Double-Decker Sandwiches.

Whatever culinary arts may be involved, however, the making of a sandwich is basically the same whatever the ingredients. From the 'tea-on-the-lawn' variety to the 'fried-egg-in-a-loaf' brand, it all starts with two slices of bread and a filling!

Very often we try to make a sandwich out of life. We take a slice of work and a slice of leisure and somewhere in between we insert our faith in God and our religious beliefs as a sort of filling.

Sometimes the whole thing holds together pretty well, but often the kind of person we are at work or at home bears very little relation to the kind of thinking we do in church.

Jesus said, 'I am the bread of life' – not the jam or the paté, mind you, but the wholesome nourishment which feeds us, makes us grow, and gives us strength to serve him every day in every situation.

It's just a thought . . .

READING

John 6:32-35

Then Jesus said to them, 'Very truly, I tell you, it was not Moses who gave you the bread from heaven, but it is my Father who gives you the true bread from heaven. For the bread of God is that which comes down from heaven and gives life to the world.' They said to him, 'Sir, give us this bread always.'

Jesus said to them, 'I am the bread of life. Whoever comes to me will never be hungry, and whoever believes in me will never be thirsty.'

PRAYER

God, our provider, we thank you for our daily bread. You are the mainstay of our lives and in Jesus we find the sustenance we need. Help us to feed upon his love and let his teaching be our staple diet.

8

Free range

How do you like your eggs? Boiled, scrambled, poached or fried? Made of china, chocolate or soap?

Farm eggs are both plentiful and cheap. Sadly we pay a price for such abundance. The cruel constraints of battery farming have led many of us to question the treatment of birds cooped up without room to spread their wings. There are many who feel it is well worth the extra expense of buying eggs which are laid by free range hens. Is it imagination to suppose that those eggs have more flavour and a better colour because they are laid by 'happy' hens?

'Free range *eggs*' is really a misnomer, conjuring up as it does pictures of eggs rolling about the farmyard enjoying themselves! It is, of course, the hens who do the ranging and in many ways they have a harder life than their battery counterparts. Searching for their own food, instead of being spoon-fed with a balanced diet, suffering the hardships of heat and cold, light and dark, instead of basking in a controlled temperature and artificial sunlight, they will face the hazards of attacks from the fox instead of the protection of the hen-house. We can only guess at which the hens would prefer.

We do know, however, which *we* would prefer. Maybe this is why God made us 'free range' individuals – giving us free will to choose how we should live our lives. Believing or denying, obeying or refusing, following or straying – the choice is ours – watched over by a heavenly Father whose only coercion is the Love that will not let us go.

It's just a thought . . .

READING

John 8:31-36

Then Jesus said to the Jews who had believed in him, 'If you continue in my word, you are truly my disciples; and you will know the truth, and the truth will make you free.' They answered him, 'We are descendants of Abraham and have never been slaves to anyone. What do you mean by saying, "You will be made free"?'

Jesus answered them, 'Very truly, I tell you, everyone who commits sin is a slave to sin. The slave does not have a permanent place in the household; the son has a place there forever. So if the Son makes you free, you will be free indeed.'

PRAYER

God, our creator, you give to your children the precious gift of free will. You do not coerce us or force us to love you. You give us the choice to follow or to go our own way. God of might and power, you do not overwhelm us, but in patience you wait for our willing response to your love. Help us to choose your way, to listen to your knock and open the door.

9

Birthday cake

Birthdays, candles and cake go together!

There is an old saying that 'you cannot have your cake and eat it'. I wonder! I think of all the children's parties we had – the mountains of jelly, sausages, crisps, peanuts, chocolate biscuits and gallons of 'Coke' that were consumed; and always when we cut the cake there were protests that everyone was too full to eat it and wanted to take it home!

And as I wrapped each slice in a paper serviette with somebody's name on it, I wondered what became of it then?

Apart from those which were unceremoniously stuffed into coat pockets, dropped on the path, squashed in the car door, or taken by somebody else by mistake, there was always one slice left behind in the hall! And what of those pieces which survived the perilous journey home? Were they thrown away? Or did they stimulate the growth of interesting bacteria in the bottom of someone's shoe bag until discovered a week or two later?

I am inclined to say that you cannot have your cake *unless* you eat it!

Which leads me to wonder what *we* do when we have a good thought, when we hear a challenge or 'get the message'? Do we wrap it up and take it home? Lose it? Forget it? Or throw it away? Or do we digest it then and there – act upon it and let God's word nourish us?

Life is for living. Cake is for eating. Perhaps the only way to *have* your cake *is* to eat it?

It's just a thought . . .

READING

James 1:22-25

But be doers of the word, and not merely hearers who deceive themselves. For if any are hearers of the word and not doers, they are like those who look at themselves in a mirror; for they look at themselves and, on going away, immediately forget what they were like. But those who look into the perfect law, the law of liberty, and persevere, being not hearers who forget but doers who act – they will be blessed in their doing.

PRAYER

God, the giver of all good gifts, we all want to share in your benevolence, and yet we do not always want the responsibility it bears. By our neglect or carelessness we squander the opportunities which come our way. Help us not only to receive but also to remember; not only to listen but also to act.

10

Out of circulation

Like a library book temporarily withdrawn, I felt decidedly 'on the shelf'. Was it really only two-and-a-half days since I took to my bed with the flu? It seemed more like two-and-a-half months. It wasn't just the aches and pains, but the little things – the pillows which wandered about the bed, the stickiness of the cough mixture bottle – and that picture on the opposite wall which was not quite straight.

I wished someone would come, and then when they did, bless them, they would arrive in droves from downstairs, sit heavily on the end of the bed, and plonk laden trays and piles of magazines all over my vulnerable limbs, then drift away leaving everything just out of reach . . . and that picture at the end of my bed was still crooked!

The bed became mysteriously full of crumbs left, I think, by the picnickers who perched from time to time around the perimeter of my pedestal, nibbling snacks while telling me how comfortable I looked and optimistically suggesting that I was improving by the hour! Strange distant sounds echoed from below – like piles of saucepans being dropped and doors blown off their hinges and whole teasets falling from high shelves. Then while no-one was about I just tiptoed to the end of the bed and put that picture straight. The first sign of recovery!

Back on my feet again I thought of those who through health or circumstance were more permanently 'out of circulation' than I had been. For when we are forced to retire to the sidelines for a time, how much we long to get back into the game!

We so readily forget the feelings of isolation and helplessness which may accompany long-term illness or disability. It is so much easier for us to *do* than to *endure*. But we can be sure that the Jesus who, through his passion, was prepared to accept what was done to him, will understand our frustration and despair in such circumstances, and will never leave us to suffer alone.

It's just a thought . . .

READING

2 Corinthians 1:3-5

Blessed be the God and Father of our Lord Jesus Christ, the Father of mercies and the God of all consolation, who consoles us in all our affliction, so that we may be able to console those who are in any affliction with the consolation with which we ourselves are consoled by God. For just as the sufferings of Christ are abundant for us, so also our consolation is abundant through Christ.

PRAYER

God of all comfort, when we are temporarily 'out of circulation' because of illness or injury, save us from irritation and self-pity. Help us to remember those whose lives are permanently affected by ill-health or disability. May the comfort of your presence strengthen us and them, and show us ways to encourage one another.

11

The bells are ringing

You have to be quick these days, don't you?

You dash downstairs to answer the doorbell only to find that the milkman has gone on his way leaving you one pint short. You stand with your ten pence piece poised over the telephone box, struggling to get more money in before you get cut off. Old people take their lives in their hands to cross the road before the little green man stops bleeping! We live our lives with our fingers on the buzzer waiting to seize the golden opportunity before it is too late. 'Hurry, hurry – offer closes tomorrow' . . . 'Sale ends Saturday' . . . 'Final notice'.

Well, maybe it is a good thing we should be kept on our toes! There is at least one sense in which it's good to 'jump to it' and act quickly. From time to time, we all have those promptings of conscience which tell us that there is something we could or should be doing. We hear an appeal, we see a need, we wonder about a neighbour and it rings a bell with us. But if we don't answer the bell, the moment has passed, the opportunity gone. It is all too easy for us to 'switch off' the alarm and to tell ourselves that someone else will answer the bell!

When we were children, my father used to say, 'Whatever you have to do, do it *now*.' I often remember his words and bless him for that sense of urgency that got things done and still prompts me in my more procrastinating moods to try to answer the bell before it rings off, perhaps for ever.

It's just a thought . . .

READING

James 4:13-17

Come now, you who say, 'Today or tomorrow we will go to such and such a town and spend a year there, doing business and making money.' Yet you do not even know what tomorrow will bring. What is your life? For you are a mist that appears for a little while and then vanishes. Instead you ought to say, 'If the Lord wishes, we will live and do this or that.' As it is, you boast in your arrogance; all such boasting is evil. Anyone, then, who knows the right thing to do and fails to do it, commits sin.

PRAYER

Lord, we do hear your voice of conscience ringing in our ears. Forgive us that so often we 'switch off' your call or delay in answering. Knowing what we should do, we find excuses. Keep us on our toes to respond right away, to serve you today in case it is too late tomorrow.

12

O ye of little faith

It was a very good programme indeed. First we switched to Channel 4 and we had mixed fill, three rinses, medium wash, automatic rinse hold and a short spin. Later we tuned into the wool programme, which gave us four rinses and a gentle action wash followed by a long spin. When we first installed our new automatic washing machine, I remember how we sat in the kitchen, watching, spellbound, as it coped with all the problems of biological stains, crease resisting finishes, and deep-down softness – without us even getting our hands wet!

I remember, too, the strange feeling of anxiety it engendered. Delegating responsibility is never easy to the conscientious worker. What was really going on in there behind the porthole door? How could I be sure that it would not leak, or boil over, or rinse before it washed? I felt I had to hover around to supervise, just in case!

Gradually I learned to let well alone and now, as in most households today, the automatic washing machine is regarded as an indispensable piece of household equipment.

It occurred to me that our faith in God is a bit like this! We say we believe in his power and love, but we still have our doubts! We pray for strength and guidance and then keep fussing around in a state of indecision about what we should do. We know that God cares, but we still worry and fret over little things.

When we put our trust in God it's even better than putting our laundry into an automatic washing machine. We can go and get on with our life with confidence, secure in the knowledge that God knows what he is doing and he will not let us down.

It's just a thought . . .

READING

Matthew 6:25-30

Therefore I tell you, do not worry about your life, what you will eat or what you will drink, or about your body, what you will wear. Is not life more than food, and the body more than clothing? Look at the birds of the air; they neither sow nor reap nor gather into barns, and yet your heavenly Father feeds them. Are you not of more value than they? And can any of you by worrying add a single hour to your span of life? And why do you worry about clothing? Consider the lilies of the field, how they grow; they neither toil nor spin, yet I tell you, even Solomon in all his glory was not clothed like one of these. But if God so clothes the grass of the field, which is alive today and tomorrow is thrown into the oven, will he not much more clothe you – you of little faith?

PRAYER

God, our protector, we do worry even though we profess to be your children. Help us to live our lives without needless anxiety. Increase our faith and help us to trust you for all that we need, secure in the knowledge of your loving care.

13

Corner shop

We used to have one at the top of our street when I was a little girl – a small grocery shop with a bell that tinkled as you pushed open the door. There was a heavy oak counter behind which rose an imposing array of tins and jars, and in front of which was a chair for the customers who sat down to discuss their needs, watched their goods being weighed into dark blue paper bags, and sampled the biscuits from the row of square glass-lidded tins arranged along the front!

It was not only the shopping list which was discussed, but the state of the world, the weather, and most importantly the welfare of the local customers – known by their names, and missed if they failed to come in regularly for their supplies. At the end of the day a boy on a bike would deliver a cardboard box containing the week's groceries, and the whole procedure was an enjoyable experience.

Perhaps you remember, too, the draper's shop where a dark-suited gentleman made a parcel of your purchases with stiff new brown paper and string, folded and tied with precision; or the dairy counter where a white-coated assistant patted the butter into neat packs; – a quarter pound, three quarters of a pound; whatever weight you required – dipping the wooden butter pats into a bowl of salt water, and leaving a ribbed pattern on each portion, making shopping into an art form.

Time-consuming? Uneconomic? Well, yes – but a million miles away from the huge glossy, streamlined supermarkets of today. Of course, we have moved on with our 'help-yourself, pick-your-own, plastic bag' philosophy, but maybe we have lost something along the way: the personal touch which was food for the spirit as well as for the body, the comforting familiarity of being served by someone who knew us and knew our needs. I spent fifty pounds in Sainsburys the other day, but nobody asked me how I was!

If you have ever tried unsuccessfully, as I did recently, all over London, to buy something of a particular size and shape, and then come home and found just what you wanted in a small local store, you will appreciate what 'shopping locally' can mean.

When it comes to our emotional and spiritual needs we are more blessed. We do not have to make a pilgrimage to Mecca, join a vast congregation, or queue up at the gate of heaven. God is at hand, waiting to serve us, knowing what we need, and caring for us as individuals.

Try shopping locally – it really works!

It's just a thought . . .

READING

Matthew 7:9-11

Is there anyone among you who, if your child asks for bread, will give a stone? Or if the child asks for a fish, will give a snake? If you then, who are evil, know how to give good gifts to your children, how much more will your Father in heaven give good things to those who ask him!

PRAYER

Bounteous God, you wait to supply all our needs, and you are ready to answer our prayers if only we ask you. We do not have to make a journey to find you for you are always close to us. We do not have to plead for your help – your bounteous love is already ours if we will accept it. We are asking, we are accepting, today.

14

Keeping fit

All over the country large ladies in leotards and lean lads in track suits are moving to music or jogging in leggings to keep themselves fit! Beautiful or breathless, muscular or miserable, the aim is the same – getting ourselves 'in condition' to make the most of life.

The experts will tell us that the secret of exercise is that it should be regular and regulated. No one attempts the marathon without a long period of training – no one dives from the top board until they have learned to swim!

Of course, it is much easier to exercise with other people. You may feel rather silly touching your toes all on your own – and in any case it's all too easy to cheat! No one will know if you bend your knees or do three instead of five; but when we join a group or exercise with a friend we encourage one another, feel fitter and have more fun!

The same rules apply to our spiritual life. I suppose it is possible to be a Christian all on your own – indeed in some communities it is necessary – but how much harder it is to hold fast to that which is good when we are perhaps the only one in the office, the school or shop who dares to try.

In order to follow in the footprints of Christ we need to practise the steps. Our exercise programme is there in the Bible, our 'warm-ups' begin with prayer, and sharing in the fellowship of the church provides the music for our movement.

By participating in the life of the church we shall be able to encourage one another and keeping fit for life will be much more fun!

It's just a thought . . .

READING

Ephesians 4:15-16

But speaking the truth in love, we must grow up in every way into him who is the head, into Christ, from whom the whole body, joined and knit together by every ligament with which it is equipped, as each part is working properly, promotes the body's growth in building itself up in love.

PRAYER

Jesus, our coach and example, let us train with you. On our own we may falter and fail; but together we can do all things. Help us to build each other up and so become fit for your kingdom.

15

The genuine article

There were so many imitators of Mr Kellogg's breakfast cereals that, in the early 1900s, Mr W. K. Kellogg put his signature on each packet. His signature became the consumer's guarantee of the highest quality breakfast cereals available and is their trademark even today. I found this out from reading the side of the Bran Flakes packet!

As consumers we are probably more conscious of quality today than ever before. We are constantly on the look out for the label which says, 'Real Leather', 'Genuine Sheepskin', 'One hundred per cent Cotton' or 'Pure New Wool'.

Food manufacturers are now required to declare themselves by an accurate description of their products – 'Real Fruit' – 'No Artificial Colouring' – 'Low Fat' – and 'Only Natural Ingredients'. Our guarantee is in their name and reputation.

I was happily munching some 'Scampi Fries' the other day when my glance fell on the packet which bore a charming picture of fishing boats at sea. I was amused to read the list of ingredients. These consisted of flavourings, colourings, emulsifiers and additives – plus, I think, a little corn and water. Certainly those fries had never seen a fishing boat, let alone a fish!

And, speaking of labels, imagine if we had to display one, what legend would it bear? 'A Real Person', 'Genuine Human', 'One hundred per cent Reliable' or 'Guaranteed Pure'? Most of us would probably be happier with 'Synthetic', 'Mixed Fibres', 'Substandard' or 'Slightly Imperfect'!

And if our label reads 'Christian', what a responsibility we bear! For Christ's signature is the guarantee of quality of life and the world will judge his kingdom by what they see in us.

It's just a thought . . .

READING

Matthew 7:15-20

'Beware of false prophets, who come to you in sheep's clothing but inwardly are ravenous wolves. You will know them by their fruits. Are grapes gathered from thorns, or figs from thistles? In the same way, every good tree bears good fruit, but the bad tree bears bad fruit. A good tree cannot bear bad fruit, nor can a bad tree bear good fruit. Every tree that does not bear good fruit is cut down and thrown into the fire. Thus you will know them by their fruits.'

PRAYER

God of Truth, whose name is above every name, you have called us your friends. Help us to be worthy of the label we bear, for your name's sake.

16

Promises, promises

Something new? Don't forget to fill in the guarantee card . . . a very interesting exercise indeed!

We have 'guaranteed' shrink-proof undies, shower-proof cagoules, dishwasher-proof crockery, heat-proof casseroles and run-proof tights; non-stick pans, non-stretch clothes-lines, non-scratch gadgets and non-flam pyjamas! What a wonderful cling-resistant, crease-resistant world we live in! It would hardly seem necessary to repair or replace anything in the guaranteed genuine society of today.

Of course, it's very important to read the small print! It's here that we find a hint of what we may expect, little gems of wisdom such as, 'The guarantee is void if the watch has been tampered with, taken apart, improperly oiled or otherwise ill-treated'; 'This guarantee does not cover defects occurring due to abuse or normal wear and tear'; 'These boots are not meant for walking'?

I was very impressed by a ballpoint pen which had a 'lifetime guarantee'. How long does a ballpoint pen live?

'To guarantee', the dictionary tells me, is 'to undertake responsibility for the fulfilment of a promise.'

Fortunately for us, God's promises are not subject to any 'escape' clauses. He did not promise that we should have a non-stick, non-scratch life, but he did promise to be with us always – not on condition that we behave ourselves and keep to the rules, but even if we abuse his plans, tamper with his universe and ill-treat ourselves and other people. His guarantee extends beyond the limits of normal wear and tear – even unto the ends of the earth.

A life-giving, lifelong guarantee of *life* from one who is Manufacturer, Supplier and Servicer of his creation.

It's just a thought . . .

READING

Numbers 23:19-20

God is not a human being, that he should lie,
     or a mortal, that he should change his mind.
Has he promised, and will he not do it?
     Has he spoken, and will he not fulfil it?
See, I received a command to bless;
     he has blessed, and I cannot revoke it.

PRAYER

God, our guarantor, we know you always keep your promises. In a world of change and uncertainty we can rely on you. We thank you that your unchanging love endures despite all our misuse of your gifts, and that your guarantee will never run out.

17

What the eye does not see

A big crowd gathered in the empty shop which was the stage for a mock auction in the High Street. Canteens of gleaming cutlery, chiming clocks, tea-sets and ten pound notes changed hands rapidly as the audience warmed to the patter of the auctioneer.

Then came the *pièce de résistance* as he offered for sale a cardboard box wrapped in brown paper. Insisting he was not allowed to disclose its contents, he suggested that for the privilege of purchasing this amazing bargain he was prepared to accept the ridiculously low figure of – not ten pounds or eight pounds – but five pounds! The crowd surged forward eagerly as they fought for the opportunity to spend five pounds on they knew not what!

It sounds incredible – but it happens. Even you and I are prepared to pay for some things we cannot see. Every time we pay our electricity bill we make an act of faith! We certainly cannot see or handle the electricity we buy – but we know it is there because we can see the effects of its use. We feel the warmth, the light and power it generates in our homes. We flick a switch and it boils our kettles, cooks our food and washes our clothes.

I believe the power of God is like the power of electricity. We cannot see or touch it, but when we make our act of faith and 'switch on' we can feel it in action – motivating, warming and energising our lives.

It's just a thought . . .

READING

Ephesians 3:14-19

For this reason I bow my knees before the Father, from whom every family in heaven and on earth takes its name. I pray that, according to the riches of his glory, he may grant that you may be strengthened in your inner being with power through his Spirit, and that Christ may dwell in your hearts through faith, as you are being rooted and grounded in love. I pray that you may have the power to comprehend, with all the saints, what is the breadth and length and height and depth, and to know the love of Christ that surpasses knowledge, so that you may be filled with all the fullness of God.

PRAYER

Almighty God, the source of all life and energy, electrify our lives from the powerhouse of your love so that we may be filled with your enabling spirit.

18

Push on

I remember the day my car broke down – in the middle of the main road – as I was waiting to turn right. In vain I tried to restart it – choke in – choke out – revving up and coaxing the ignition. Traffic passed me on both sides and I began to feel rather embarrassed, very inadequate and decidedly vulnerable until a kind young van driver, realising my predicament, leapt from his cab and cheerfully volunteered to give me a push into the comparative safety of the service road.

After some expert advice, a good blow into the petrol tank, and a little rock-and-roll on the bonnet, the offending bit of dirt in the carburettor was apparently dislodged, and I was mobile once more.

We all need a bit of a push sometimes! When the engine is sluggish or the electrics fail, we find ourselves resorting to that most primitive source of energy – a hearty push!

The dictionary defines 'push' as 'to urge forward', 'to impel', 'to carry on vigorously'. It's a push which gets the grass cut, vacuums the carpet and pedals the bike uphill.

Sometimes we need a spiritual push too. We have a good intention, we dream a splendid dream, but ideas are volatile and dreams fade. We need the motivation which turns thought into action and prayers into practice. We need someone to 'give us a push'.

A word of encouragement, a helping hand, a vote of confidence – these may urge us forward to greater effort, to persevere with a difficult task or sometimes, when we have stalled, to start all over again!

And by far the best kind of push is still a pat on the back!

It's just a thought . . .

READING

Hebrews 10:23-25

Let us hold fast to the confession of our hope without wavering, for he who has promised is faithful. And let us consider how to provoke one another to love and good deeds, not neglecting to meet together, as is the habit of some, but encouraging one another.

PRAYER

Give us a push, Lord, when our motivation stalls! You are our strength and our inspiration. Your love impels us to persevere. Above all help us to encourage one another and so keep travelling on.

19

Keep it simple

I hate gadgets! Food choppers which dismantle into sixteen parts for washing up – instead of just one knife! Knitting machines which require you to sit up and learn to play the organ instead of relaxing in an armchair with a pair of needles and a ball of wool! Wrist-watches which play a tune and make toast as well as telling you what the weather is like in Timbuktu. And when you have to study the small print to find out how to open a tin of sardines, I think we have gone too far!

I have this strange aversion to gimmickry – the art of making simple tasks complicated.

I like things which just do what they are designed to do, without having to go on a course to understand the instructions!

Modern technology has brought many miracles to our door but life has become much more complex as a result. I wonder sometimes if we have similarly complicated our spiritual lives? Could it be that there are too many conflicting doctrines and rituals, rules and regulations?

Jesus certainly didn't issue any fifty-two page leaflets on 'How to enter the kingdom of heaven'! Instead he spoke about bread, and seeds, and sheep, and fishes. He told us that we should become like children, and his new commandment was that we should love God and our neighbours as ourselves.

If only we could take him at his word, wouldn't life become much more simple, more straightforward and more joyous, too?

It's just a thought . . .

READING

Matthew 11:25-26

At that time Jesus said, 'I thank you, Father, Lord of heaven and earth, because you have hidden these things from the wise and the intelligent and have revealed them to infants; yes, Father, for such was your gracious will.'

PRAYER

Lord, save us from complications! Forgive us when we make them an excuse for not following your commandments, or when we put stumbling blocks in the way of others. Give us the childlike faith which aims to 'keep it simple'.

20

Communications

When one of my children was small she was asked by Grandma, 'What did you do at school today?' 'Nothing much,' she replied. 'Cracking nuts?' was Grandma's astonished response! These famous words have been immortalised as a family joke in which Grandma was always happy to share. They do illustrate, however, how misunderstandings can arise from a breakdown in communications.

In the course of my work I came across a remarkable piece of equipment designed to assist conversation with those who are hard of hearing. It was called a 'Communicator' and consisted of a small microphone connected to a receiver which could be held to the ear. A communicator provided that link between speaker and listener and made for better understanding all round.

In the world today we are more in need of good communications than ever before. Sadly we still shout at one another rather than discuss, and when talks break down there is conflict instead of communion.

In the church we are all 'communicants', for I was interested to discover that to 'communicate' also means 'offering worship', but could it be that sometimes we have failed to communicate? Have we truly forged that link between the church and the community which welds together worship and work, concern and caring, prayer and practice, and makes our neighbourhood an extension of God's kingdom?

My 'Communicator' was a valuable aid to successful interviewing, but it needed to be fuelled by a battery, to be switched on, and to be taken out to clients who needed it.

So do we.

Our battery is God's love in our hearts. We are switched on by enthusiasm for his work and our readiness to take that love out to those who need it.

It's just a thought . . .

READING

Isaiah 61:1

The spirit of the Lord GOD is upon me,
because the LORD has anointed me;
he has sent me to bring good news to the oppressed,
    to bind up the brokenhearted,
to proclaim liberty to the captives,
    and release to the prisoners.

PRAYER

Lord God, the author of good news, show us how to communicate your love. When our lines of transmission break down, reconnect us to your supply. Teach us how to understand and be understood. Join us together in communion with you and with the people we meet day by day.

21

Part-timer

Glancing down the Situations Vacant column in the local paper, I was intrigued by the different kinds of 'person' required. There were vacancies for a 'bright and intelligent young person', a 'reliable person', an 'active person', a 'mature person', an 'ambitious person', a 'qualified person' and a 'supervisory person'! Most amazing of all was the advertisement for a 'part-time person'. Now what, I wondered, is a part-time person for the rest of the time when they are not being a person?

The dictionary defines 'person' as 'a human being as distinguished from . . . an inanimate object', 'a human being having rights and duties' or 'an individual possessed of personality'. And yet there is a sense in which we are all part-timers.

On a wet Monday morning a visitor from another planet might be forgiven for mistaking us for inanimate objects, and it is often easier to forgo our rights and duties than to exercise them! Sometimes we experience a moment of uplift during an inspiring service, or if we perform an heroic deed. For a while we live our lives on a higher plane – possessed of personality indeed. But often these moments fade in the humdrum of everyday life. It is not always easy to be a 'person' when we are washing-up or weeding the garden. So which part of our time are we really being a person? Is it only when we feel inspired and fulfilled?

To be a whole person means to be valued and loved. The greatest gift we can give our children is the knowledge that we love them. This is what God does for us.

Jesus said, 'I am with you always' – not from 10.30 to 11.30 on Sunday mornings, or when we are taking Communion, but *always*: when we get up in the morning, on the bus to school, when we get home from work and when we go to bed.

His presence makes every moment count. He transforms our part-time effort into full-time fellowship with him; the secret of being a whole person and not just a part-timer!

It's just a thought . . .

READING

Matthew 10:29-31

Are not two sparrows sold for a penny? Yet not one of them will fall to the ground apart from your Father. And even the hairs of your head are all counted. So do not be afraid; you are of more value than many sparrows.

PRAYER

Dear God, you have shown how much you love and value us. In your great compassion you accept us with all our faults and shortcomings, not just on our better days, but throughout our lives. We thank you for your unreserved love which makes us whole and gives us full-time fellowship with you.

22

Look at the picture

Struggling to understand the instruction book for my new sewing machine, I was startled to read:

> Changing foot: Raise pressure foot lifter. Bring needle to highest position.
> Push button of holder towards you and foot will come off.

I'm happy to say that it didn't, and that I still have two feet firmly on the ground! This was followed by two pages of instructions for threading the needle, a procedure which, in practice, took only seven seconds!

My sandwich toaster manual was more explicit:

> The wire which is coloured GREEN and YELLOW must be connected to the terminal in the plug which is marked with the letter 'E' or coloured GREEN. The wire which is coloured BLUE must be connected to the terminal which is marked with the letter 'N' or coloured BLACK. The wire which is coloured BROWN must be connected to the terminal which is marked with the letter 'L' or coloured RED.

Well, I guess anybody would have known that!

Written instructions can be, and often are, confusing, complicated and contradictory. Diagrams help but are not always clear. Photographs point the way, but a personal demonstration is the most effective of all.

The religious leaders of Jesus' day were experts at reading instructions. They knew the intricate details of the Law. Their knowledge of its history and teaching could not be faulted. They were so steeped in procedures that somehow they managed to miss the whole point.

Jesus came to simplify the Law – to bring a new Law of *love* into our lives. His instructions were clear and precise: 'Follow me.' He spoke, he listened, he healed and helped and prayed. He understood and forgave. He demonstrated his teaching to the very limits of love by laying down his own life and forgiving his enemies, even from the cross.

If we really want to be part of God's kingdom, we need look no further than this: 'They that have seen me have seen the Father.'

It's just a thought . . .

READING

1 Corinthians 2:1-5

When I came to you, brothers and sisters, I did not come proclaiming the mystery of God to you in lofty words or wisdom. For I decided to know nothing among you except Jesus Christ, and him crucified. And I came to you in weakness and in fear and in much trembling. My speech and my proclamation were not with plausible words of wisdom, but with a demonstration of the Spirit and of power, so that your faith might rest not on human wisdom but on the power of God.

PRAYER

We read the instructions and we are bewildered.
We study the map but we are still confused.
But we look at you, Lord, and we can see the way.
Help us to follow you.

23

Three bags full

We must be a nation of bag-carriers! Sitting on the promenade at Eastbourne, watching the world go by, we were astonished by the quantity of luggage which the Great British Public lugs around with it on holiday.

Beach bags, shoulder bags, holdalls and hampers – there seems no limit to the equipment we find necessary for a day by the sea.

Speculation as to what was in the bags provided a hilarious half-hour. Spare socks, fishing rods, newspapers and knitting; bags of books, buns and bandages, cameras, carpets and canteens of cutlery – if it's portable it seems that we will 'port' it!

Children who wouldn't carry a packet of crisps home from the shops were to be seen humping great buckets of stones from one breakwater to another. Old ladies and gentlemen, weighed down with winter coats and thermos flasks, struggled with an umbrella in one hand and an ice-cream cornet in the other. Teenagers yanked enormous radio-cassette players, and Mums and Dads, like walking hat-stands, disappeared down the zigzag path to the sands bearing all the rest of the family's worldly goods!

What is this obsession with carrying things around?

It probably has something to do with the notion that we must be prepared for any emergency – rain or shine, hot or cold, hunger or thirst. But when emergencies do arise it's not what's in the bag that will enable us to cope, but the strength and inspiration which comes from God – our inner resource. It is the power of his presence which encourages us to persevere and his love which sustains us through our darkest days.

It's just a thought . . .

READING

Matthew 10:7-10

As you go, proclaim the good news, 'The kingdom of heaven has come near.' Cure the sick, raise the dead, cleanse the lepers, cast out demons. You received without payment; give without payment. Take no gold, or silver, or copper in your belts, no bag for your journey, or two tunics, or sandals, or a staff; for labourers deserve their food.

PRAYER

Help us to travel light, Lord, as we journey for you. May we be ready to put down our baggage and put all our trust in you.

24

Stop, look and listen!

'Look at me when I'm talking to you!' – words many of us will have said to our nearest and dearest! British Telecom once launched an advertising campaign to get us to communicate more, pointing out that in the animal world lifelong partners never stop talking to each other. In many households a few words thrown over a shoulder before the door slams: 'I'll be late tonight!' or 'Dinner ready?' which often pass for conversation, or the cursory 'Where are my blue socks?' with the reply 'Where you left them!' shouted down the stairs, hardly constitute the true meeting of minds!

Most Methodists do not find any difficulty in talking to one another; the problem is usually in getting us to stop! But the general hubbub of chatter in which we indulge before and after (if not during!) the Sunday service is no substitute for real discussion and sharing of thoughts. In order to understand the problems and anxiety, the hopes and joys we experience as individuals and as a church, we do need to communicate.

And what about when we talk to God? Is 'Let us pray' sometimes the signal for us to wonder if we switched the oven on or locked the car? Or maybe to present God with a long list of requests or complaints?

Maybe the secret of prayer lies in those words with which we began – God saying to us, 'Look at me when you are talking to me.' For if we do stop and look at God as shown to us in Jesus, the distractions and trivialities will surely disappear and many of our questions will be answered without the need for words.

It's just a thought . . .

READING

John 14:8-9

Philip said to him, 'Lord, show us the Father, and we will be satisfied.' Jesus said to him, 'Have I been with you all this time, Philip, and you still do not know me? Whoever has seen me has seen the Father. How can you say, "Show us the Father"?'

PRAYER

Lord, we are looking at you. In you we see the answers to our prayer. In you we see God's love for us and for the world. In you we see the way that we should go. Make your face to shine upon us and be gracious unto us, we pray.

Sunflowers

The sky was full of sunshine and the fields were full of sunflowers as far as the eye could see. The whole landscape was illuminated by pools of gleaming gold as we drove southwards on our grand tour of France. Sunflowers are amazing when seen *en masse* at the height of their glory, all turning their faces with one accord – towards the sun. Then, as they absorb the light and warmth, their heads become heavy with ripening seeds and each bloom becomes a miniature factory, producing the oils and vitamins which will later be harvested and transformed into health-giving spreads for our bread and our cooking.

Sunflowers, natives of Central America, are now widely grown in a number of South American and EC countries and always they look to the sun. We have now learned how to reap the benefits for a blooming generation (apologies to the advertisers of a well-known product!).

Maybe you have never thought of yourself as a flower? Many of us would more likely see ourselves as a vegetable: a hearty cabbage, a sturdy oak, or maybe just a nut! But there is a sense in which I believe we can emulate the sunflower.

Just as plants which are deprived of light will soon wilt and fade, we also need light to enable us to grow in love and understanding. God's goodness, like the sun, shines down on us and it is when we turn towards it and allow its wonderful energising power to enrich our lives that we can go on to process it in the service of others.

It's just a thought . . .

READING

Psalm 84:11-12

For the LORD God is a sun and shield;
    he bestows favour and honour.
No good thing does the LORD withhold
    from those who walk uprightly.
O LORD of hosts, happy is everyone who trusts in you.

PRAYER

Shine on us, Lord, and turn our faces towards you, so that the light of your love may enrich us and the power of your Spirit may enable us.

26

Smoothing things over

Having just finished the ironing I feel I have good cause to rejoice! The room is pleasantly pervaded by the aroma of warm, fresh laundry. Shirts dance on their hangers, crisp and clean, and most importantly, I can now see the bottom of the wicker basket once again!

Some things are easy to iron. I have always had plenty of offers to 'do the square ones'! It was the one hundred per cent cotton blouses with tucks, the linen tablecloth with lace, and – worst nightmare of all – the denim dungarees with dried-in creases which gravitated to the bottom of the heap and stayed there! Some would say ironing is a waste of time. Everything soon gets all screwed up again, so why do we do it? Is it because we feel that a crumpled appearance may give the impression of a crumpled personality? Most of us find that in order to feel good we need to look good too!

The mistakes we make in our lives are a bit like creases in the laundry. They spoil the line, are uncomfortable to wear and proclaim to the world that we have fallen short. But it sometimes takes more than a hot iron to eradicate the scars. Maybe we just try to 'smooth things over' on the surface, but still feel regret and pain underneath. Perhaps what is needed is a complete rewash! When we have hurt others we need the opportunity to make reparation. Like Peter after his denial of Jesus, we need to be able to meet our Lord on the shore of the lake, to reaffirm our love, and then, in the assurance of his forgiveness, to do something practical by taking up his commission to carry on his work.

It's just a thought . . .

READING

John 21:15-17

When they had finished breakfast, Jesus said to Simon Peter, 'Simon son of John, do you love me more than these?' He said to him, 'Yes, Lord; you know that I love you.' Jesus said to him, 'Feed my lambs.' A second time he said to him, 'Simon son of John, do you love me?' He said to him, 'Yes, Lord; you know that I love you.' Jesus said to him, 'Tend my sheep.' He said to him the third time, 'Simon son of John, do you love me?' Peter felt hurt because he said to him the third time, 'Do you love me?' And he said to him, 'Lord, you know everything; you know that I love you.' Jesus said to him, 'Feed my sheep.'

PRAYER

We are sorry for the mistakes we have made, Lord, and most of all for the hurt we have caused you. We find it hard to forgive ourselves. We thank you that you not only forgive us, but also give us the opportunity to make reparation by renewing our service for you.

27

About time

On my way to the station the other day, as I hurried to catch a train, I heard a voice from above asking, 'Have you got the time, love?' I am not usually given to hearing voices. My faith, imperfect though it is, relies more upon the promptings of my heart and mind. However, being startled into a response, I glanced upwards only to see a workman repairing the roof overhead beaming down on me and tapping his wrist! 'Oh! Er, yes, it's a quarter to two,' I stammered and hurried on my way. So much for my angelic messenger! But it set me thinking again 'Have I got the time .. ?'

Time is a very elusive concept. We always seem to have either too little or too much! It is possible to keep it, waste it, make it, lose it or spend it, but we never seem to have enough time to do all the things we would like to do.

1995 was, for many of us, nostalgia time as we remembered the days of the war with its privations, tragedies, challenges and triumphs. In those days we were ever aware that time was precious. With the shadow of disaster hanging over us, we lived for the present, grateful for small mercies and for our very survival from day to day.

In the realms of eternity it is only 'quality time' that really counts. A few moments spent doing the things we really enjoy or being with the people we love are more precious than any number of hours spent in aimless pursuits or frustrating waits. The most important thing is how we spend our time. Do we have time to listen and to talk to one another? Time to stand and stare at the wonders of God's world?

One thing is certain: our living Creator God is not bound by the limits of time. He 'was and is and is to be for aye the same'. God always has time for us. Do we have time for him?

It's just a thought . . .

READING

Ecclesiastes 3:1 and 11

For everything there is a season, and a time for every matter under heaven:
He has made everything suitable for its time; moreover he has put a sense of past and future into their minds.

PRAYER

God of eternity, you always have time for us. Help us to spend our time wisely and well and always find time to be with you.

28

Breakfast

What do you like for breakfast?

Do you favour the 'breakfast-in-bed-with-a-rose-in-a-vase-on-a-tray' variety? Or have you a secret yearning to help yourself to kidneys or kippers or kedgeree from a silver dish on the sideboard? The traditional British breakfast of bacon and eggs, sausages and fried bread, tea, toast and marmalade has been superseded in many cases by fruit juice and cereal with semi-skimmed milk. Breakfast invariably sets the tone for the day and, as dieticians are agreed, we neglect it at our peril!

Some breakfasts hold special memories: delicious white rolls with black cherry jam and coffee on a balcony in Switzerland; or the smoky aroma of 'eggy bread' on the dew-damp grass at Guide Camp. Early morning picnic breakfasts of bacon and egg sandwiches with coffee in a flask *en route* to the seaside were the prelude to holiday joys. What a way to start the day!

And there we have it . . . the association of ideas which the first meal of the day encapsulates. It had been a long night for the friends of Jesus, fishing under the dark skies without a catch. As they pulled ashore in the grey light of dawn, they saw the glowing embers of a little fire. Maybe the appetising smell of grilled fish wafted towards them even across the water. And Jesus said to them, 'Come and have breakfast.' What a way to start the day!

After that blessed reunion, breakfast would never be the same again!

It's just a thought . . .

READING

John 21:4-6 and 9-12

Just after daybreak, Jesus stood on the beach; but the disciples did not know that it was Jesus. Jesus said to them, 'Children, you have no fish, have you?' They answered him, 'No.' He said to them, 'Cast the net to the right side of the boat, and you will find some.' So they cast it, and now they were not able to haul it in because there were so many fish.

When they had gone ashore, they saw a charcoal fire there, with fish on it, and bread. Jesus said to them, 'Bring some of the fish you have just caught.' So Simon Peter went aboard and hauled the net ashore, full of large fish, a hundred and fifty-three of them; and though there were so many, the net was not torn. Jesus said to them, 'Come and have breakfast.' Now none of the disciples dared to ask him, 'Who are you?' because they knew it was the Lord.

PRAYER

Friend of the fishermen, make yourself known to us. To you we look for food, for fellowship and forgiveness, knowing that you can provide them all.

29

Lost for words

A visit to the stationers in search of a greetings card is almost like embarking on a course of higher education. By the time you have selected the classification, the gender, the words and the picture and tracked down the chart to enable you to decipher the cost code, you are too weak to change your mind and start again!

These days it is possible to buy a card for almost any occasion. Greetings range from 'Happy Mother's Day to my cousin's wife' or 'Merry Christmas to a favourite milkman' to 'Congratulations on your failure to catch chicken pox'! The difficulty arises if your cousin hasn't got a wife or if it was measles you failed to catch. Hooray for the section headed 'Blank – for your own message'.

Words do not always say what we want them to. There are many situations in life when we find it difficult to express ourselves. We are *speechless* with horror, *tongue-tied* with embarrassment and when life's great crises of tragedy or joy come our way, words are quite inadequate.

Perhaps we should not let this worry us too much. The world is, inundated with talk. Every day great torrents of words flow out into the atmosphere from both radio and television. The world is full of committees, councils and conferences. There is never a shortage of words. Platitudes, promises, premises and prejudices all come pouring out.

Maybe we need fewer words and more understanding. There is consolation in this thought for those who find it hard to communicate. Sometimes the very fact of being there, of a kindly action, or a reassuring glance can be more telling than a thousand words.

It's just a thought . . .

READING

Proverbs 25:11-13

A word fitly spoken is like apples of gold in a setting of silver. Like a gold ring or an ornament of gold is a wise rebuke to a listening ear. Like the cold of snow in the time of harvest are faithful messengers to those who send them; they refresh the spirit of their masters.

PRAYER

Word of God, you became flesh and lived among us. We saw your glory, full of grace and truth. Speak through our lives, we pray, so that when we are lost for words, we may communicate your love by our actions.

30

Carry on caring

'It's going on all the time,' we say with a sigh as we put down the newspaper or turn off the television news. Wars, disasters, vandalism, violence . . . sometimes it seems that there is no end to the problems of the world.

'It's going on all the time,' we say when we hear of broken marriages, child abuse and drug or drink-related disasters.

'It's going on all the time,' we say when we hear of old people dying of neglect, babies abandoned and animals being exploited for profit. The evils of society could so easily become a recipe for despair.

On a recent visit to our local hospital, I stepped into another world. A world where the battle against illness and suffering is being fought night and day. We take it for granted; in fact we are scarcely even aware of it until we ourselves, or someone close to us, are admitted for treatment. Then suddenly we realise that it is going on all the time: the skill and devotion of doctors, nurses and surgeons, the compassion and caring of people who feel that it is all worthwhile.

Babies are being born, lives are being saved, sight restored, pain relieved. New hope is being given through new health, not only near to home, but also throughout the world, because of the dedication of those workers who never give up, no matter how unequal the struggle may appear.

It's good for us to remember that the sun shines after darkness, day comes after night, God cares about his world and this too 'goes on all the time'.

It's just a thought . . .

READING

Matthew 11:2-5

When John heard in prison what the Messiah was doing, he sent word by his disciples and said to him, 'Are you the one who is to come, or are we to wait for another?' Jesus answered them, 'Go and tell John what you hear and see; the blind receive their sight, the lame walk, the lepers are cleansed, the deaf hear, the dead are raised, and the poor have good news brought to them.'

PRAYER

God, our pain-bearer, you sent Jesus to show how much you care. You never give up on us. Help us to carry on caring too, so that this world may be healed with your love.

31

Move on!

'Eighty pence a ride!' called the showman collecting fares for the carousel, while the brightly painted horses followed each other round and round on their gilded poles.

'Running on the spot, be-e-e-e-gin!' said the PE teacher to his reluctant pupils, whilst in the gym the fitness enthusiasts pedalled away on their exercise bikes.

Plenty of movement there – but not, you will agree, a lot of progress! Just moving about can certainly help to keep our circulation going, but what is even more important is the direction in which we move. To be *on the move* is one thing; to *move on* is another!

In law not only is 'loitering with intent' a crime but just 'standing around' can also be an offence! If we cause an obstruction we are blocking the way of progress.

Maybe as individuals we should ask ourselves whether we are *moving on*? When Jesus said to his friends, 'Follow me', he pointed ahead to the way which would take them out into the world around them to face the challenge of their times. In the same way he calls us to address the problems of our society today.

If we would follow him we must surely be prepared to 'take up our beds and walk', for progress (to quote the dictionary) is 'a moving forward, advance, growth and development'.

Off we go then – move along there, please!

It's just a thought . . .

READING

1 Timothy 4:14-16

Do not neglect the gift that is in you, which was given to you through prophecy with the laying on of hands by the council of elders. Put these things into practice, devote yourself to them, so that all may see your progress. Pay close attention to yourself and to your teaching; continue in these things, for in doing this you will save both yourself and your hearers.

PRAYER

Keep us on our toes, Lord, and save us from stagnation. Give us the faith which moves mountains and the vision to go forward with you.

32

Man the pumps!

We all scrambled out of the car to admire the view. A beautiful lake stretched out before us, reflecting the surrounding mountains in the stillness of the evening. So quiet and peaceful – miles away from anywhere. But we still had a long way to go so we all clambered back into the car. We had travelled only about ten yards when the car stopped. The starter turned the engine to no avail so the bonnet was raised, the boot opened and out came the toolbox, but it was no good. What a delightful place to break down – so quiet, so peaceful – but miles from anywhere! Suddenly the lake took on a different aspect when we considered the possibility of spending the night beside its darkening waters.

We finally decided we must have run out of petrol (a phenomenon difficult to explain with the gauge showing a quarter full). When our spare can of petrol was poured into the tank, the sudden inflow of fuel seemed to do the trick and we were on our way once more.

Later investigation revealed that the problem was not a lack of petrol but a faulty fuel pump. *The petrol was there but it was not getting through.*

There is enough goodwill in the world to get us well on our way to solving many of the world's problems but sadly this reservoir often remains untapped. If the pumps are not working the world goes in want.

In response to appeals the gifts pour in, but they need to be carried out again to others before the act of love is complete.

There is a great wealth of talent and compassion in Christian communities. Have we the imagination to 'man the pumps' so that the fuel of our faith can flow to the neighbourhood around us?

It's just a thought . . .

READING

Matthew 9:35-38

Then Jesus went about all the cities and villages, teaching in their synagogues, and proclaiming the good news of the kingdom, and curing every disease and every sickness. When he saw the crowds, he had compassion for them, because they were harassed and helpless, like sheep without a shepherd. Then he said to his disciples, 'The harvest is plentiful but the labourers are few, therefore ask the Lord of the harvest to send out labourers into his harvest.'

PRAYER

Lord of the Harvest, let us join your workforce. Use all our skills in your service and employ us usefully for you.

33

Can you hear me?

We all do it. When someone is a little deaf, we repeat ourselves a little louder. When someone is not tuned into our wavelength, we turn the volume up in the hope that somehow we will break the sound barrier and *get through* to them by bombarding them with noise. We even convince ourselves that anyone can understand our language if it is spoken loudly enough!

I heard someone speak about their hearing aid in this way: 'It makes everything *louder* but not *clearer*. It's just as though everyone is speaking a foreign language!'

With apologies to Lewis Carroll, one might say:

'Will you speak a little plainer?' said a whiting to a snail,
'I'm a little hard of hearing, and it's blowing up a gale!
I thought you spoke in English, but although your voice
    is loud,
To me it sounds like Japanese that's chanted by a crowd.
I have a little trouble, for your diction is not clear,
And the more you try to shout at me, the less I seem
    to hear!'

There is, of course, a subtle difference between *hearing* and *listening*. The dictionary tells us that to hear is to 'understand by listening'. The secret is in that word 'understand'. So much of what we hear today is just *noise*. Everyone thinks they will get their way if they just shout a little louder.

Fortunately for us, God does not bellow at his universe! His is the 'still small voice' that speaks to our hearts and makes his message plain. May he grant us the 'listening ear', and the understanding to pass his message on.

It's just a thought . . .

READING

1 Kings 19:11-13

Now there was a great wind, so strong that it was splitting mountains and breaking rocks in pieces before the Lord, but the Lord was not in the wind; and after the wind, an earthquake, but the Lord was not in the earthquake; and after the earthquake a fire, but the Lord was not in the fire; and after the fire a sound of sheer silence. When Elijah heard it, he wrapped his face in his mantle and went out and stood at the entrance of the cave. Then there came a voice to him that said, 'What are you doing here, Elijah?'

PRAYER

Voice of God, speak to our hearts, we pray. We live in a world of noise and clamour and so often your message is drowned out by the din of our daily lives. Help us to hear with that inner ear, and hearing, to understand.

34

Who cares?

London Underground apologises for any inconvenience caused to passengers on the Northern Line last night. The delay was due to a person falling in front of a train at Clapham South.

Commuters hurried past this notice displayed outside the station with scarcely a backward glance. It seemed very thoughtful of London Underground to take the trouble to explain the delay. It must indeed have been inconvenient for those Northern Line travellers – but perhaps not anything like so traumatic as for the unknown *person* who was so inconsiderate as to fall in front of the train.

We cannot begin to know the anguish of that unnamed person. We can only imagine the agony of the family and friends who had to endure the shock, loss and maybe the guilt.

Such is the state of our society that we have been conditioned to hear news of tragedy and disasters involving thousands of lives with little more than a shake of the head and barely a pang of regret. And when a *person* falls in front of a train we apologise for the *inconvenience*! Are we really just numbers in a book to be written off in this way?

Surely this is where our Christian belief has a reassurance for us which no other faith can give. It is like putting our hand into the hand of a friend to hear again these words of Jesus:

'Are not two sparrows sold for a penny? Yet not one of them will fall to the ground apart from your Father. And even the hairs on your head are all counted. So do not be afraid; you are of more value than many sparrows.'

Worth so much, in fact, that God sent Jesus, not only to live for us, but to die for us too, to show us how much he cares.

It's just a thought . . .

READING

Isaiah 49:13-16

Sing for joy, O heavens, and exult, O earth;
break forth, O mountains, into singing!
For the Lord has comforted his people,
and will have compassion on his suffering ones.
But Zion said, 'The Lord has forsaken me,
my Lord has forgotten me.'
Can a woman forget her nursing child,
or show no compassion for the child of her womb?
Even these may forget, yet I will not forget you.
See, I have inscribed you on the palms of my hands;
your walls are continually before me.

PRAYER

Lord, there are times when we feel forsaken, times when we wonder if anyone cares. And yet we remember your assurances that we are all valuable in your sight. Write our names on the palms of your hands, we pray; enfold us in the arms of your love and use us to show others that you care.

35

Does it work?

Have you heard about the amazing levitating pen? I quote from the catalogue: 'Place the pen on its stand and watch it 'float' without any visible means of support. Give it a gentle spin and it clearly demonstrates the interactional relationship between magnetism, gravity, friction, the chaos theory and rotational inertia. (It also makes a delightful pattern)'. What more could a good pen do?

The only thing I wondered about was – does it *write*?

We are all familiar with 'interactional relationships' – better known as getting on with each other. We are aware of the magnetism which draws us towards some people or some ideals. Gravity keeps our feet on the ground. Friction and chaos are no strangers to our lives, and certainly we are all capable of going round in circles getting nowhere (rotational inertia?). I am not so sure whether we always make a delightful pattern!

If we look to our faith as a means of giving our lives and the life of the world a 'lift', how shall we know whether we have got it right? One of the tests may be to ask ourselves truthfully, 'Does it work?' Does our faith make us more loving, more patient, more compassionate, more tolerant and forgiving, more honest, more hopeful and happier? Are we willing to believe that God cares for each one of us and has a purpose for every life, even those of whose life style we do not approve? Do we have confidence that God is with us and with them in every kind of sorrow and danger?

As Christians we make many professions of faith but it is only when that faith can be seen in action that our calling is truly fulfilled.

It's just a thought . . .

READING

1 Corinthians 13:4-8

Love is patient; love is kind; love is not envious or boastful or arrogant or rude. It does not insist on its own way; it is not irritable or resentful; it does not rejoice in wrongdoing, but rejoices in the truth. It bears all things, believes all things, hopes all things, endures all things. Love never ends.

PRAYER

Jesus our Lord, you have shown us how love works. You have not asked us to follow a theory but to put our faith into action. You have given us the tools; help us to use them for you.

36

Mystery action

The gleaming red and gold train – a replica of a midwestern American steam engine – was in a big cellophane-fronted box. 'This is just what I really, really wanted!' said our little grandson as he unwrapped it on Christmas morning. 'It's got real smoke . . . and mystery action,' added his Dad, quoting the instructions. 'Oh no!' was the incredulous response, 'not *mystery action*!' The ensuing laughter set the tone for the rest of the day.

In this case, the 'action' was battery-operated – one more hazard to negotiate as I contrived to cook the Christmas dinner with three excited children weaving in and out of the kitchen in pursuit of the train, a helicopter and a mini doll's pram.

Every time I pick up the telephone or the TV remote control or produce a printout from the computer, I am aware of the 'mystery actions' which operate in our world today. Things scarcely dreamed of thirty years ago are now accepted as part of everyday life. And still I don't altogether understand how they work!

I have never forgotten a sermon in which the minister spoke of the house martins that returned each year to nest under the eaves of his house. How these tiny birds made a journey of several thousand miles to return home in the spring was a mystery indeed – but they did! And he likened this to our trust in God. We do not always understand how it works, but it does.

When we look at our war-torn and troubled world it is easy to despair. But when reason and logic appear to fail we should not forget that the *mystery action* of God's love in our lives can and does bring about changes beyond our wildest dreams.

It's just a thought . . .

READING

Job 11:7-9, 12:7-10

Can you find out the deep things of God?
Can you find out the limit of the Almighty?
It is higher than heaven – what can you do?
Deeper than Sheol – what can you know?
Its measure is longer than the earth,
and broader than the sea.
But ask the animals, and they will teach you;
the birds of the air, and they will tell you;
ask the plants of the earth, and they will teach you;
and the fish of the sea will declare to you.
Who among all these does not know
that the hand of the Lord has done this?
In his hand is the life of every living thing
and the breath of every human being.

PRAYER

Mysterious God, you are beyond our understanding, and yet all around us we see the evidence of your power and love. Help us to trust you to do the things we cannot do, and when our human contrivings fail, to put our concerns into your hands.

37

It can be done!

I empathised wholeheartedly when recently I overheard an exasperated mother say to her child, 'Don't argue – *just do it!*' How many times have I resorted to the same command?

When we stand contemplating a difficult task, wondering where to begin, or when we have walked away from a problem that is seemingly insoluble, we might do well to follow that advice ourselves.

We are all guilty at times of arguing ourselves out of a difficult situation. We hear that someone has been bereaved but persuade ourselves that it would be a mistake to visit because we might not know what to say. Or we hesitate to bring people together because we fear there may be differences of opinion, or we might upset someone. We want to help the starving children of the world but we tell ourselves the money might never get there, or that our small effort would not make any difference.

So often we find that moves towards Christian unity are thwarted by obstacles of dogma and detail. Meetings and committees discuss and debate, but their deliberations are often abortive. But when God's people of all denominations come together in a crisis or celebration his Holy Spirit moves among them, regardless of sect or schism, to unify the whole. *It can be done!*

When Jesus called his disciples he simply said, 'Follow me', and they did! No elaborate negotiations, no documentation, just a spontaneous response to a call of love. If we truly believe that we are in tune with God's purposes we can afford to follow the impulses of our hearts, knowing that he will enable us to cope with the consequences. No ifs and buts please – *just do it!*

It's just a thought . . .

READING

Ephesians 3:20-21

Now to him who by the power at work within us is able to accomplish abundantly far more than all we can ask or imagine, to him be glory in the church and in Christ Jesus to all generations; forever and ever. Amen.

PRAYER

Enabling Spirit of God, forgive us, we pray, for the times when we prevaricate, when, ignoring the promptings of your Spirit, we make excuses; when we allow petty arguments to stand in the way of action. Help us to listen to your voice, to trust in your guidance and when something needs to be done, to *just do it!*

38

Umbrellas

What go up when the rain comes down? Umbrellas! Fringing the golf course like exotic blooms – umbrellas! Jostling for room on the crowded beach, brilliant and brash – umbrellas! Along the river-bank, cool and green, sheltering the anglers – umbrellas!

Derived from the latin *umbra* meaning shade, this symbol of protection has been adapted for many needs. You may like to know that your friendly umbrella is really 'a portable device for protection against rain, snow or sun, and consists of a light canopy supported on a collapsible metal frame mounted on a central rod'! More than this, the umbrella has given its name to 'any system or agency that provides general cover for a group of related companies – an umbrella group'.

Some people see the Christian church along these lines – an 'umbrella group' sheltering us from the realities and hardships of life. In fact we know that our faith in God is not designed to 'shield' us from the difficulties of life, but rather to overcome them.

I remember a poster produced by a large insurance company which depicted a packet of umbrella seeds and a subsequent harvest of umbrellas. God does not provide us with umbrella seeds but with the seeds of his kingdom which like the mustard seed will grow into a great tree. Jesus was probably referring to the black mustard, the seeds of which were used for oil as well as flavouring, and which can grow as tall as fifteen feet, providing shelter for many birds.

When conditions become severe umbrellas are liable to collapse or blow away. But as the leaves of a tree are able to survive the rain, so the power of God's love enables us to combat the storms of life – a protection which far surpasses the shelter of an umbrella.

It's just a thought . . .

READING

Mark 4:30-31

He also said, 'With what can we compare the kingdom of God, or what parable will we use for it? It is like a mustard seed, which, when sown upon the ground, is the smallest of all the seeds on the earth; yet when it is sown it grows up and becomes the greatest of all shrubs, and puts forth large branches, so that the birds of the air can make nests in its shade.'

PRAYER

We do not ask you to shelter us from life's storms, Lord, but by the power of your love to make us weatherproof.

39

Are you 'in condition'?

A little drop of conditioner will give you Deepdown Softness, Lasting Freshness, Less Static Cling and Fewer Wrinkles! It helps prevent damage, restores balance and leaves you shiny, bouncy and manageable. It's marvellous how we can be restored, retextured and rejuvenated for just a few pence extra at the supermarket.

We can recondition washing machines, renovate soft furnishings, recharge our batteries, recycle our rubbish or reclaim waste land. With the right treatment we can put new life into our material world. But how about a *spiritual* conditioner? Sadly we have sometimes used the wrong kind! We have allowed ourselves to be conditioned to accept things the way they are – the way they have always been – and in so doing, our mission has become less relevant to the needs of today. In the same way we may have become conditioned to regard the ills of society as inevitable, and have lost the enthusiasm for crusade.

What we need is the kind of conditioner which will revitalise our faith, replace the static with the dynamic force of empowering love – a pouring out of God's Holy Spirit into our lives to enthuse us afresh with joy.

It's just a thought . . .

READING

Psalm 51:10-12

Create in me a clean heart, O God, and put a new and right spirit within me. Do not cast me away from your presence, and do not take your holy spirit from me. Restore to me the joy of your salvation, and sustain in me a willing spirit.

PRAYER

God, our maker and our motivator, pour out your Holy Spirit on us, we pray, so that reconditioned and refreshed we may be always looking for new ways to serve you.

40

Don't call us . . .

Whether you are applying for a job, a passport or a new cheque book, you may be sure that there will be a form to complete. School reports, market surveys, questionnaires – sooner or later you will be asked to tick the box, cross out which doesn't apply, or complete the tear-off and return.

You may well be invited to write (in BLOCK CAPITALS) your name, address and date of birth in minute spaces for anything up to a dozen times, with other long-forgotten particulars of your history for the benefit of ICI, BBC, DSS or any number of Government departments. Best of all is the section on the form where you are invited to explain your reasons for the application, or to answer with due modesty the astonishing question, 'What makes you think you can do this job?'

And then, when you have described what a knowledgeable, competent and conscientious member of society you are, and how your every waking moment is filled with good works, you may be invited for an interview at which you will be given the opportunity to answer hypothetical questions and share your hopes and aspirations with a panel of total strangers, only to be told, 'Don't call us – we'll call you!'

How fortunate it is that we need no such form-filling to become followers of Jesus! He does not require particulars of our circumstances, examination papers or means tests. He already knows us better than we know ourselves, and when he calls us it is just to say he loves us and wants us to share his love.

It's just a thought . . .

READING

Psalm 139:1-4

O Lord, you have searched me and known me.
You know when I sit down and when I rise up;
you discern my thoughts from far away.
You search out my path and my lying down,
and are acquainted with all my ways.
Even before a word is on my tongue,
O Lord, you know it completely.

PRAYER

God, the great employer, you have vacancies for all. When we apply to you, we can forget the paperwork, for you already know us as we are and as we hope to be. By your almighty power you can use us with all our imperfections. Help us to hear your call and work for you.

41

Do you see?

Why is it that the pen you keep by the telephone is always missing when you need it?

An elderly lady told me a story about this. She was watching television one afternoon when an appeal was made for donations to a very good cause, but before she could write down the telephone number it disappeared from the screen. At first she was upset and disappointed until, with a flash of genius, she wrote down her own telephone number in large figures and held it up to the screen asking the presenter to 'phone *her* instead!

Not such a strange idea when you think about it, for how many times at the end of a programme have you heard someone say, 'That's all for tonight – we'll *see* you at the same time tomorrow.'

But there is a kind of *seeing* that has nothing to do with *sight*: an 'inner' seeing which means we understand and believe. Often people worry and doubt because their religious experience does not seem real enough. 'I say my prayers but I do not hear any answer,' they say or, 'I have never seen a vision like the prophets or disciples.' Even Thomas said, 'Unless I see I will not believe.'

Perhaps the important thing is not that we are ever able to see God – for nobody has – but that he sees *us*, his children, cares for us and reveals himself to us in the teachings of Jesus, who said, 'Blessed are those who have *not* seen and yet have come to believe.'

It's just a thought . . .

READING

John 20:24-29

But Thomas (who was called the Twin), one of the twelve, was not with them when Jesus came. So the other disciples told him, 'We have seen the Lord.' But he said to them, 'Unless I see the mark of the nails in his hands, and put my finger in the mark of the nails and my hand in his side, I will not believe.'

A week later his disciples were again in the house, and Thomas was with them. Although the doors were shut, Jesus came and stood among them and said, 'Peace be with you.' Then he said to Thomas, 'Put your finger here and see my hands. Reach out your hand and put it in my side. Do not doubt but believe.' Thomas answered him, 'My Lord and my God!' Jesus said to him, 'Have you believed because you have seen me? Blessed are those who have not seen and yet have come to believe.'

PRAYER

Immortal, invisible God, grant us the insight to recognise you, to walk by faith and not by sight, and to believe without seeing.

42

Blight or blossom

My team of young would-be gardeners wanted to know 'which are the weeds?' A good question, indeed – for who decides? How is it that the sunny-headed dandelion and the delicate pink convolvulus are designated 'weeds' while speedwell and kingcup are revered as 'wild flowers'?

The dictionary definition is intriguing:

> *Weed*: a useless or troublesome plant in cultivated land, a plant springing up where it is not wanted in a garden etc; any useless or troublesome, intrusive thing.

However it is interesting to note that even a weed has its uses. The dandelion, so often despised by gardeners is a favourite food of our tortoise; its young leaves make a tasty salad when blanched, and the cooked green leaves are an alternative to spinach. The roots are used in some countries as a coffee substitute and the flowers make a good wine. It has a wide application as a medicine and provides valuable nectar for bees. Even the stinging nettle is food for the caterpillars of the very loveliest butterflies. The young leaves provide food for goslings and ducklings, and are a rich source of vitamin C. Some comfort here for those of us who see ourselves as humble herbs rather than exotic blooms!

Sometimes we are tempted to make judgements about other people, but we need to be careful about designations! Surely we can leave the weeding to the one who created us and knows us all, wheat and tares alike.

It's just a thought . . .

READING

Romans 14:10-13

Why do you pass judgement on your brother or sister? Or you, why do you despise your brother or sister? For we will all stand before the judgement seat of God. For it is written, 'As I live,' says the Lord, 'every knee shall bow to me, and every tongue shall give praise to God.' So then, each of us will be accountable to God. Let us therefore no longer pass judgement on one another, but resolve instead never to put a stumbling block or hindrance in the way of another.

PRAYER

God, the Gardener, you created our world and saw that it was good. You have implanted in each one of us the potential to live and grow. Only you know the undeveloped value of our lives. Help us humbly to tend your garden and leave the harvesting in your hands.

43

Sponsored walk

Our five-year-old grandson has just completed a sponsored bounce – sixty-two bounces in one minute on a bouncy castle – in aid of some new school equipment. Our society is becoming ever more fitness-conscious, and with a big boom in aerobics, exercise classes and workouts, it is good to know that all this energy is being put to doubly good use when it is linked with the sponsorship of good causes.

With sponsored swims and sponsored silences, sponsored press-ups and sponsored jogs, sponsored sit-ins and sponsored knit-ins, those of us who are diffident about actively taking part can salve our consciences by sponsoring someone else to stand on their heads on our behalf!

In its true form, however, sponsorship means much more than 'ten pence a mile or £5 the lot'! It can be defined as 'a surety – one who undertakes to be responsible for another, a godparent or a guardian; someone who will watch over us and provide support for us'.

The idea of life being a journey is familiar to us all. Walking is to some a great pleasure, to others a great difficulty, and to many a great bore! But a walk can always be transformed by the company we keep on the way. When we are walking with friends and talking as we go, we do not notice how long or difficult the road may be.

Best of all, if we walk with God then life can be a *sponsored walk* in the true sense of the word.

It's just a thought . . .

READING

Proverbs 4:10-12

Hear, my child, and accept my words,
that the years of your life may be many.
I have taught you the way of wisdom;
I have led you in the paths of uprightness.
When you walk, your step will not be hampered;
and if you run, you will not stumble.

PRAYER

Jesus, you are the Way. In your company we are surefooted on the roughest path. Grant us your sponsorship through life's journey and the security of following in your footsteps.

44

Take 2

There was great excitement in the office in anticipation of a visit by a VIP. Desks were tidied, waste bins emptied and only the red carpet was missing! An enthusiastic amateur photographer undertook to record the occasion for posterity and, assembling his impressive equipment, he followed the entourage from one section to another as the visitor progressed through the department. Shaking hands, drinking tea, asking questions . . . nothing was left out. Half-way round he ran out of film and hastened to put a new one in his camera.

A few days later, as the staff waited expectantly to see the prints, the awful truth was revealed – every one was a 'double take'. In his enthusiasm, the photographer had inadvertently replaced the old film in the camera instead of the new one, and had taken another set of pictures on top of the old. Not a great success!

In our personal or church life, we are sometimes inspired to make a fresh start. Perhaps we have heard a great speaker, or have come through a traumatic experience; maybe we have formed a new relationship or started a new job. Suddenly we feel the need to put our hopes or desires into action. We want to enrich our lives and change the world. But so often we simply put the old film back in the camera and run it all over again. The same old mistakes and disappointments are repeated and all we have is a succession of double takes!

Jesus told us it was no use patching an old coat with new material or putting new wine in old bottles. If we really want to make changes, we must not be afraid to be drastic, for with a new film in the camera, we may just take the picture of a lifetime.

It's just a thought . . .

READING

Matthew 9:16-17

No one sews a piece of unshrunk cloth on an old cloak, for the patch pulls away from the cloak, and a worse tear is made. Neither is new wine put into old wineskins; otherwise, the skins burst, and the wine is spilled, and the skins are destroyed; but new wine is put into fresh wineskins, and so both are preserved.

PRAYER

God of re-creation, show us how to begin again. Save us from repeating past mistakes and give us the courage to make a new start.

45

Getting in touch

'This is your Captain speaking.' The voice of the pilot came through our headphones to tell us we were cruising at thirty-five thousand feet over the Atlantic on our journey to the USA. At the same time we were able to watch Thames TV News on the screen before us!

We picked up a telephone in an isolated mountain resort in Pennsylvania and dialled fourteen digits to put us in immediate contact with home, and held a conversation that was as clear as if we had been in the same room. Such are the wonders of modern science that we take these everyday miracles in our stride.

A few days later we were being driven along a freeway when we noticed that the truck in front of us had a wobbly wheel. Our host immediately picked up his CB radio and enquired of the lorry ahead, 'Hey, Schreiber, have you got your ears on?' and alerted him to the danger. Those words amused us at the time and have haunted me ever since.

Many people may be trying to get in touch with us – by speech, by phone, by the written word or maybe by a silent plea. The world is crying out for compassion and concern. Have we got *our* ears on? Sometimes we strive to get in touch with God. We struggle to find the right words to say to him, the right petitions to make. We worry about how to get his attention, and sometimes we think he doesn't hear as we bombard him with requests. Perhaps we should relax and just listen! Maybe God is trying to get in touch with *us*! God does not need a telephone or radio to speak to our hearts, but he does say, 'He who has ears to hear – let him hear.' Have we got our ears on?

It's just a thought . . .

READING

1 Samuel 3:8-11

The Lord called Samuel again, a third time. And he got up and went to Eli, and said, 'Here I am, for you called me.' Then Eli perceived that the Lord was calling the boy. Therefore Eli said to Samuel, 'Go, lie down, and if he calls you, you shall say, "Speak Lord, for your servant is listening." ' So Samuel went and lay down in his place. Now the Lord came and stood there, calling as before, 'Samuel! Samuel!' And Samuel said, 'Speak, for your servant is listening.' Then the Lord said to Samuel, 'See, I am about to do something in Israel that will make both ears of anyone who hears of it tingle.'

PRAYER

Voice of God, speak to us, we pray. Grant us the grace to have our ears switched on when you get in touch with us. Help us to listen to your words and to do what you would have us do.

46

Stay switched on!

A small green card dropped through our letter-box to warn us that our water supply had failed, and for the next few hours we lived in a state of suspense trying to think of things to do which did not involve turning on the tap! The obvious things like having a bath or using the hose were not too difficult to come to terms with, but when we realised that we could not readily make a cup of tea, rinse sticky fingers or even brush our teeth, we really began to feel inhibited.

Have you ever filled the kettle, wondered why it took so long to boil, and then realised that it was not switched on? Or experienced a power cut when time itself stood still in the form of an electric clock?

We live in a marvellous age when power lies at our fingertips. With the flick of a switch we are connected to vast resources of energy – and equally easily the supply can be disconnected.

As I was leaving the church the other day, I was stopped in my tracks by a notice on the hall door which read 'SWITCH OFF WHEN YOU LEAVE'! In God's house, whether it be for worship or service, or simply for fun, we are connected to the main source of his power and glory. Challenged by words from the Bible, a message from the preacher or simply warmed by the fellowship we find there, we are stirred to go out and put our thoughts and prayers into action.

What a pity if all that divine energy and inspiration is to be switched off when we leave! So my message would be: 'On these premises we can reconnect our lives to the source of all love and power – *DON'T* SWITCH OFF WHEN YOU LEAVE!'

It's just a thought . . .

READING

Hebrews 13:15-16

Through him, then, let us continually offer a sacrifice of praise to God, that is, the fruit of lips that confess his name. Do not neglect to do good and to share what you have, for such sacrifices are pleasing to God.

PRAYER

God eternal, the mainspring of all goodness, when we close the book, when the amens are said, when we leave your house, keep us at all times switched on to your truth, ready and willing to serve.

47

Sun-day!

It was a dark and dismal morning. Low clouds overhead threatened further rain and the pavements beneath our feet were leaden grey. Heads were bowed, collars turned up, lips pursed and eyes cast down as commuters and shoppers trudged on their way. Then suddenly the sun came out! Glinting on the inky puddles, where oily rainbows formed, reflecting on car windows and lighting up the sky, the welcome rays transformed a winter's scene. The effect was miraculous as with lightened steps and cheerful smiles the travellers moved on.

We all need sunshine. Like plants, people who are deprived of it wilt and become sad. Indeed the medical profession now recognise that some people are physically affected by the lack of sun.

Sunshine is an instant tonic. If we cannot find it on the weather map we create our own sunshine substitutes – sun-ray lamps, sunshine breakfasts, sunflower margarines, sun-silk shampoos and sun-fresh washing up liquid! Sunshine warms our hearts and lifts our spirits. It brings out the best in us and makes us grow. Sunshine sustains life!

We cannot, of course, change the weather, but there is another source of sunshine which is not dependent upon the time of year or the day of the week. God's love is like sunshine. Education sheds light upon the world so that we can learn and understand its workings. Moral codes shine like stars to give guidance and purpose to our lives. But in the cold light of reason there is still something missing. Only the love of God gives sunshine to the world. Sunshine is catching – smiles bring smiles – warmth generates warmth – and the good news gets around!

If Christianity is to grow it must be full of the spiritual sunshine that will radiate through our lives to the lives of others, making each and every day a Sun-day.

It's just a thought . . .

READING

Numbers 6:24-26

The Lord bless you and keep you;
The Lord make his face to shine upon you,
and be gracious to you;
The Lord lift up his countenance upon you,
and give you peace.

PRAYER

Shining love of God, light up our lives with your radiance. Warm our chilly hearts with your graciousness, and dazzle us with your hope.

48

Mind the doors!

Doors are intriguing and exciting – you never know what you may find behind them. Some doors are formidably closed – like Fire Doors kept shut to prevent the spread of flame. Some are heavy to open – as you will know if you have stood patiently and politely holding one while all the world troops through! Revolving doors can take you out again before you have really been in.

On holiday in Italy we found a treasury of history and art, but much of its beauty was behind closed doors. Walking along a narrow street between tall buildings with plaster crumbling on the walls, paint peeling from the windows, decaying wooden shutters and very little light to relieve their drab exteriors, we would suddenly come upon an open door and there, inside, would be a cool green oasis – a little courtyard with fountains, palms and exquisite flowering shrubs. Or, entering a church which looked closed and neglected, we would find a sanctuary adorned with gold, marble, colourful mosaics, paintings and statues glimmering in the soft candlelight, surprising even the casual visitor with a sense of wonder and worship.

Jesus said, 'I am the door.' What a wonderful imagery this conjures up: a 'means of access' to eternal truth, and a way into the kingdom of God.

I should like to think that the doors of our churches symbolise his message, saying to those outside, 'All are welcome to come in' and to those within, 'Go out into the world, and God be with you.'

It's just a thought . . .

READING

John 10:7-9

So again Jesus said to them, 'Very truly, I tell you, I am the gate for the sheep. All who came before are thieves and bandits; but the sheep did not listen to them. I am the gate. Whoever enters by me will be saved, and will come in and go out and find pasture.'

PRAYER

Jesus, the doorkeeper of our destiny, bless our comings and goings, and help us to find the way into your kingdom.

49

Skin deep

They had to be 'whole, fresh in appearance, sound, clean, practically free from any foreign matter, well-developed and free from unhealed injuries . . .' So read the specifications. What were we talking about? The criteria for an art exhibition? A beauty contest? Or a model agency? No! Believe it or not these were the EU standards for horticultural produce – common standards of quality for Class 1 sweet peppers. Furthermore the width of the sweet peppers should not be less than: elongated (tapering) 30mm; square sweet peppers (blunt) 50mm; and flat sweet peppers 55mm! So now you know how hard it is for a sweet pepper to find its way on to the supermarket shelves!

We have all grown accustomed to fruit and vegetables which are visually perfect – shiny and shapely, without blemish or blight – but could it be that their beauty is only skin deep? Gardeners know that home-grown tomatoes with all their variations in size and colour will often taste sweeter than those in a plastic pack. Adverse publicity about chemical sprays and fertilisers has prompted a move towards more natural, organic growing methods. For the sake of healthy eating and flavour we may become more discerning in our selection and be more ready to accept the misshapes.

It is fortunate for us that the standards set down for a Christian life are not based on our size or colour or shape. If we were to be judged by appearances, many of us would be rejected out of hand! Mercifully God does not discriminate, as we sometimes do, against those who do not clean their shoes or get their hair cut. We have only one standard of perfection against which to measure our fitness for his kingdom, and that is personified in Jesus; in his life, his words, his teaching and his example. And through the eyes of God we may behold the beauty of the soul.

It's just a thought . . .

READING

Galatians 5:22-23

By contrast, the fruit of the Spirit is love, joy, peace, patience, kindness, generosity, faithfulness, gentleness and self-control. There is no law against such things.

PRAYER

God of all goodness and beauty, behold us with all our imperfections. Only you can discern the potential of our lives. Grant us the faith which is more than skin-deep and help us to be fruitful for you.

50

New – Improved!

Do you enjoy your breakfast cereal? Is it crunchier, munchier, maltier and more 'full of country goodness' than the others you have tried? Are you satisfied with your washing powder? Does it give you a cleaner, brighter, whiter wash? Does your dog like his dinner – is it meatier, chunkier, tastier than before? Look around your supermarket and you will find kitchen rolls that are longer, stronger, more absorbent; cleaners that go deeper; flour that is lighter; 'New Recipe', 'New Formula', 'New Fragrance', 'New Size' and 'New-improved'.

It can be disconcerting to discover that commodities we have grown to know and love have been changed. 'New Fragrance' may not have the same comforting ambience we expect. 'New Recipe' may alter a flavour we particularly enjoy, and 'New Size' may simply mean 'smaller'!

Most of us move cautiously towards change. The same can be said about our spiritual experience. If we have grown up in a Christian environment there will be words of scripture, stories and hymns which are as familiar to us as breathing; traditions of worship which have become a way of life. The people of Jesus' day who had been taught in the synagogue would also have been steeped in the heritage of their Jewish faith. When Jesus came it was not to do away with that heritage but to build upon it. His teaching was to throw new light and meaning on the word of God by making it relevant to their daily lives, 'a new-improved' revelation of God's love.

Although it may be unsettling we should never be afraid to step away from tradition, to question and to search for new meaning in the tenets we hold dear. Sometimes it takes a new version to shock us into an awareness of what God is saying to us. Results will tell us whether we have got it right. Are our lives brighter, more hopeful, more purposeful, more helpful than before? Only then will we be able to say whether the 'new' is 'improved'!

It's just a thought . . .

READING

John 13:34-35

Jesus said, 'I give you a new commandment, that you love one another. Just as I have loved you, you also should love one another. By this everyone will know that you are my disciples, if you have love for one another.'

PRAYER

Jesus, our example and our enlightener, shine anew in our hearts. Keep us always looking for new ways to serve, new people to love, new meanings in your word and a new, improved way of living for you.

51

Losers

'Where have you put the car keys?' 'Who has taken my umbrella?' 'Has anyone seen the paper?' 'What has happened to the nail scissors?'

Is there a familiar ring to these questions? Are you a 'loser' too? Then join the club! On reflection many of us spend a high proportion of our waking lives searching for things that we, or others, have mislaid. Not only do we burn up precious energy in retracing our steps but even more in frustration when we cannot find what we are looking for.

There is, of course, a useful formula which sometimes brings results. We try to remember where and when we last saw it, what we were doing at the time, and, logically, we may be led to recover it. On the other hand, it is often only when we have given up the search that we come across the missing item quite by chance in an unexpected place – possibly when we are looking for something else.

Society is not very tolerant of its losers, generally branding them as irresponsible or weak. Whether we lose our tools, our jobs or our way, it is often assumed that we have somehow been neglectful, careless or just plain stupid.

Finding *ourselves* is an altogether different matter. Many of life's problems are blamed on heredity or environment, and the 'cure' is directed into searching for causes in the long distant past. Jesus had a very different answer: 'Those who find their life will lose it, and those who lose their life for my sake will find it.'

Those who care for other people more than themselves – such as the busy parent nursing a sick child, or the family looking after an elderly relative – seem to be able to rise above their own problems in a very special way. Similarly, members of the accident and emergency services, who disregard their own safety, find themselves rising to the occasion with a God-given strength which surmounts all difficulties. The answer may well be in looking outwards rather than inwards and by losing ourselves in the service of others to let God do the finding!

It's just a thought . . .

READING

Matthew 16:24-26

Then Jesus told his disciples, 'If any want to become my followers, let them deny themselves and take up their cross and follow me. For those who want to save their life will lose it, and those who lose their life for my sake will find it. For what will it profit them if they gain the whole world but forfeit their life? Or what will they give in return for their life?

PRAYER

Jesus, in the eyes of the world a loser, you gave everything for us. Keep us for ever looking outwards instead of inwards and help us to see that it is only by losing ourselves in the service of others that we can truly find ourselves.

52

What's new?

Happy New Year!

Wonderful as Christmas is, there comes a time when we are glad to take the decorations down, to clear up the endless pine needles, the bits of walnut shell and tinsel which find their way into the corners of the room, between the cushions, and into such unlikely places as the dog's basket and Dad's slippers. Then we can make a fresh start!

By now most of us will have eaten all the 'soft centres', washed with the new soap, worn our new gloves, written cryptic messages in our diaries, and made our first mistakes! Already the pristine newness will be ever so slightly tarnished, and like the first footprints on the untrodden snow, our daily living will have made its mark on the New Year.

'What a shame,' you may say. 'Wouldn't it be lovely if things could remain for ever new?' But don't despair: there is a sense in which God's world *is* ever new! For being a Christian means that we live from one moment to the next in the knowledge that whatever may have happened ten years ago, ten days ago – ten minutes even – we can still start again this very instant! We don't have to wait until New Year's Day comes around to make good resolutions. The first of January or the thirty-first of July are both alike to God!

When a very dear 'Auntie' celebrated her ninetieth birthday, she was asked what she would like for a present. She replied, 'I'd really like a modern English dictionary! I keep hearing new words on the television and I like to know what they mean!'

If we can keep that sense of wonder through the years then time will have no dread for us, and every day will be the first day of the rest of our lives!

It's just a thought . . .

READING

Lamentations 3:22-23

The steadfast love of the LORD never ceases,
    his mercies never come to an end;
they are new every morning;
    great is your faithfulness.

PRAYER

God of new beginnings, we see the evidence of new life all around us. Each day we discover new wonders and new hope. Each day you renew your love for us. Help us to face the future unafraid, knowing that whatever we have done or left undone, it is never too late to make a fresh start.

53

Memorabilia

I heard on the radio one day that a group of elephants on their way to Russia were being detained in Holland because they did not have the necessary papers with them!

What a scene that conjures up! Mother Elephant searching frantically through her handbag, Father turning out his pockets, and the kids all trumpeting madly because it's lunchtime and they want to be on their way! Were they required to unpack their trunks? Papers? Passports? How could they have been forgotten? Elephants never forget!

Memory plays many tricks on us, especially as we grow older, when we may be able to recall the most intricate details of our childhood but are quite unable to remember what we did yesterday afternoon. I'm sure that most of us will have experienced the frustration of not being able to recall a name or a number which is just 'on the tip of our tongue'. On the other hand, some of us could no doubt confess that occasionally we have used our memories as a convenient excuse! I wonder if it is true that we only remember what we choose to remember.

Psychologists reassure us that an occasional lapse in memory or absence of mind is nothing to worry about, but is perfectly normal in those who lead a busy life. What is more important, perhaps, is the *quality* of what we remember!

There are quite a lot of elephants around! How often have you heard 'Of course I have forgiven them – but I shall never *forget*.'

The start of a New Year is always a nostalgic time. What kind of memories shall we take with us into the coming months? I would like to think that we shall choose to remember only what is pure and lovely and of good report, and that our forgiveness from God and towards each other is complete.

It's just a thought . . .

READING

Philippians 4:8-9

Finally, beloved, whatever is true, whatever is honourable, whatever is just, whatever is pure, whatever is pleasing, whatever is commendable, if there is any excellence and if there is anything worthy of praise, think about these things. Keep on doing the things that you have learned and received and heard and seen in me, and the God of peace will be with you.

PRAYER

Loving keeper of our memories, you have given us minds to think and hearts to love. Let us not forget to give you thanks and praise. Guard our thoughts from everything that would separate us from you, remembering only what your love has taught and forgiving others as we are forgiven.

54

Making music

It was New Year's Eve and we sat in hushed expectancy in the great concert hall at the Barbican Centre as the members of the London Symphony Orchestra took their places on the platform and began 'tuning up'. Slowly there arose a great cacophony of sound as the strings and woodwind, brass and timpani vibrated into life in a few moments of discordant chaos. Then, as the noise died away and silence fell, the conductor took his place. One could have heard a pin drop. The conductor raised his baton, and suddenly the great hall was filled with melody.

The transformation was miraculous, the audience entirely captivated, and those same instruments which had previously produced one vast conglomerate of noise now spelled magic for us.

It made me think again of how we, with our varying gifts and talents, are like an orchestra. Sometimes we are late coming in, out of tune, sharp or flat. Sometimes we miss the beat or are so busy blowing our own trumpet that we drown the finer tenor of the strings. Sometimes we are distracted and miss our cue, and often, through lack of sensitivity, we fail to interpret the Composer's meaning. We need to be led, to be inspired and to be in tune with one another. Left to our own devices we are capable of producing only disharmony, but under the baton of a great Conductor perhaps even we can make music.

The concert was for me a thrilling and uplifting experience, but hardly had the overture to the New Year begun before there was discord among the nations and disharmony in our everyday lives. We cannot rewrite the score, but if we keep our eyes on Jesus we can be sure that he will conduct us through the symphony of the coming year with the joy and understanding that God the Composer intended.

It's just a thought . . .

READING

Psalm 33:1-5

Rejoice in the LORD, O you righteous.
    Praise befits the upright.
Praise the LORD with the lyre;
    make melody to him with the harp of ten strings.
Sing to him a new song;
    play skilfully on the strings, with loud shouts.
For the word of the LORD is upright,
    and all his work is done in faithfulness.
He loves righteousness and justice;
    the earth is full of the steadfast love of the LORD.

PRAYER

God of harmony, your world is full of music. Oceans and rivers, wind and rain, the voices of children, the sound of laughter; all are orchestrated to sing your praise. By ourselves we are capable only of making a noise, but when we look to you to conduct our works, we can produce melody. You, the Composer, have inspired the music; help us to keep our eyes on your baton and faithfully to interpret the score.

55

Selfishdges

The January sales are over – but never fear – they will soon be followed by a 'Spring Event' and a 'Half Price Bonanza' which will see us through to the 'End of Season Reductions', the 'Summer Sales', the 'Autumn Clearance', and whoops! – we're back to Christmas!

Who can resist a bargain? Sales, alas, do not bring out the best in us. Queue all night – the doors open – and it's 'everyone for themselves'.

'Selfishdges – there's no place like it!' (if a certain famous store will excuse my corruption of their jingle).

'The young people of today are selfish,' say the older generation. 'They think only of themselves.' At a time of life when everyone urges you to make the most of your talents and opportunities, is it any wonder if someone gets trampled underfoot in the rush?

The middle-aged are not immune. They have lost that first fine careless rapture which counts the world well lost for love. They are guilty of 'respectability'. They do not want their little world disturbed.

So, as we grow older, do we then grow wise? Not necessarily! The trip to 'selfishdges' still goes on. One would expect that experience of life would make us more understanding of the needs of others. In fact, in many cases, our world shrinks even smaller. With the lack of mobility and motivation we draw the curtains a little closer and our thoughts turn more and more inwards.

But there is a 'Way out'. God, through his Office of Fair Trading, makes a 'Once-for-all-time offer': 'To those who will forget themselves and follow me, I will give the kingdom.' That is a bargain!

It's just a thought . . .

READING

Luke 9:23-25

Then he said to them all, 'If any want to become my followers, let them deny themselves and take up their cross daily and follow me. For those who want to save their life will lose it, and those who lose their life for my sake will save it. What does it profit them if they gain the whole world, but lose or forfeit themselves?'

PRAYER

Jesus, you gave everything for us. Help us to see that it is only by losing ourselves in service to others that we can gain true life from you. Keep us for ever looking outwards instead of inwards and change 'everyone for themselves' into 'everyone for others'.

56

March winds

From my kitchen window I can glimpse the washing line where shirts and blouses toss their arms in a wild fandango as the March wind blows through them. They tug and pull at the line – pleading with the pegs to release them – straining to be free to fly over the rooftops into the great sky beyond – and sometimes I long to fly with them!

We all find ourselves pegged down at some time in our lives. The March wind blows and we long to be free; to travel, to explore, to follow the pursuits of our hearts and to escape from the routines of life, but we are pegged down in many ways. Sometimes it is by lack of resources or opportunities; sometimes by responsibilities to our families or our jobs.

The strange thing is that often, when we do at last achieve our 'freedom', we don't know what to do with it! Many retired people confess that they look back longingly to the days when they were tied to routine and the needs of others. Pull out the pegs, and those shirts which danced so lightly in the wind will quite likely fall in the mud.

Perhaps the truth is that the only real freedom we can know is the freedom to rise above the restrictions and inhibitions of our daily lives and see the *whole* of life as a great adventure. Let the winds of the Spirit blow into our souls, refreshing and uplifting us but keeping us pegged securely to the lifeline of love!

It's just a thought . . .

READING

Deuteronomy 30:19-20

I call heaven and earth to witness against you today that I have set before you life and death, blessings and curses. Choose life so that you and your descendants may live, loving the LORD your God, obeying him, and holding fast to him; for that means life to you and length of days, so that you may live in the land that the LORD swore to give to your ancestors, to Abraham, to Isaac, and to Jacob.

PRAYER

Lord, our strength and stay, the wind blows where it pleases and sometimes we long to fly with it! In the midst of our restlessness, we pray, keep hold of us and keep us holding on to you.

57

April showers

I have just come in from shopping, shaking the drops from my umbrella all over the spattered step and wishing someone would invent windscreen wipers for spectacles!

What does a shower mean to you? To the weather forecaster it is a symbol on the map which looks like a cloud crying! To some of us it is a group of people who do not quite come up to expectations – a collection of 'drips' perhaps?

To me at the moment showers are like 'good works'. Hail showers which lash against the window and bounce on the cement with relentless purpose are like the people to whom the doing of good work is a duty; the sort of people who insist on doing good to others whether they want to be done good to or not. Their efforts are usually short and sharp and if they are received with suspicion, their good works dry up as quickly as a hailstorm, sometimes leaving a sting in the tail!

Occasionally, however, we have snow showers in April. Unexpected and romantic, they transform the world with beauty – for a brief hour. They are like the people who perform their good works lightly and casually when the mood takes them, drifting into the lives of others with good intentions only to melt away again when things get tough. Their 'good works' are gift-wrapped and splendid, but lack staying power.

But when the spring rain falls gently and steadily, feeding the thirsty plants, softening the ground and promoting health and growth, I think of the quiet people who do not perform 'good works' at all, but simply 'work for good'. These are the people whose genuine kindly interest in those around them leads them to care for others with understanding and constancy. Long may they 'rain'.

It's just a thought . . .

READING

Ezekiel 34:26-27

I will make them and the region around my hill a blessing; and I will send down the showers in their season; they shall be showers of blessing. The trees of the field shall yield their fruit, and the earth shall yield its increase. They shall be secure on their soil; and they shall know that I am the LORD, when I break the bars of their yoke, and save them from the hands of those who enslaved them.

PRAYER

Giver of life, your blessings fall like rain upon us and your continuous care overshadows all our lives. Give us the constancy to work for you in unassuming ways, sharing your goodness with others day by day.

58

If only

There we were, feeding the ducks – a delightful activity which never fails to charm children of all ages. Parents and grandparents held on to the belts and reins of the small benefactors who, perching precariously on the edge of the pond, bestowed their largesse upon the ever-eager recipients, and in their enthusiasm nearly threw themselves into the water along with their crusts and crumbs!

As Easter approaches we can look forward to the advent of baby ducks, families of ten or twelve balls of fluff bobbing about in procession behind their parents: some keeping close, some straying off into murky corners among the reeds; all being consistently and caringly rounded up by their mothers, anxious to keep them from harm.

For me one of the most poignant pictures of Jesus in the New Testament is the occasion when, gazing over the city, he cried, 'O Jerusalem, Jerusalem . . . how often have I longed to gather your children, as a hen gathers her brood under her wings; but you would not let me.'

The anguish of watching those we care for heading for disaster, rejecting our advice and our love, is surely one of the hardest things to bear. How much more so for the God who created us, and whose vision for us is for a world of beauty and fulfilment, to watch as we tear ourselves and each other apart and destroy what he has given us?

This rejection must cause as much pain in the heart of God as the cruel crucifixion caused physical agony. But still his love will not let us go.

It's just a thought . . .

READING

Isaiah 53:3

He was despised and rejected by others;
    a man of suffering and acquainted with infirmity;
and as one from whom others hide their faces
    he was despised, and we held him of no account.

PRAYER

Dear Lord, how can you still love us when we hurt you so much? Forgive the wilfulness that refuses to accept your love. Forgive us for we know not what we do.

59

The road to everywhere

The sky was heavy with black clouds which hurled themselves along before a squally wind. The rain lashed down with all the force of hail. Motorists put their headlights on. Harassed shoppers struggled with wet baskets and umbrellas. Children stepped in puddles and felt the cold wetness seep into their shoes. The brief promise of spring had been temporarily forgotten in the chill of a heavy shower. Spring can be harsh and uncompromising.

I walked along the road feeling cold and shivery, damp and uncomfortable, problems on my mind. As I started up the hill I glanced towards the grassy bank beneath the barren trees. A sudden gleam of sunlight filtered through the clouds, lighting up the gold and purple crocuses which grew along the verge like intricate embroideries on a tapestry. Someone had planted them to form the word EASTCOTE. From the hard clay soil of winter they lifted their shining heads to remind us of the new life on its way, and of the presence of God's handiwork here in the small town in which we live and move and have our being.

I thought of that other road we read of at this Easter time – the road to Emmaus, where two friends walked and met Jesus on the way; and I was glad that God still speaks to us as we go about our daily routine, that we can still feel his presence when we shop, or talk with friends, or go into the Post Office, or sit down together for a coffee. For surely if he walked along the road to Emmaus then we cannot doubt that he will walk along the road to Eastcote, or Enfield or wherever you live now, and our hearts can be warmed by simply knowing he is with us still.

It's just a thought . . .

READING

Luke 24:13-16

Now on that same day two of them were going to a village called Emmaus, about seven miles from Jerusalem, and talking with each other about all these things that had happened. While they were talking and discussing, Jesus himself came near and went with them, but their eyes were kept from recognising him.

PRAYER

Jesus, our companion, walk with us we pray. When we are wandering, when we are wondering, help us to recognise your presence and turn to you wherever we may be.

60

The bonus

The shop windows are full of Easter eggs, beautifully packed in their brilliant cardboard boxes. Eggs filled with cream and chocolate drops, eggs tied with ribbon bows, sitting in egg-cups, tea-cups, baskets and buckets; clasped by bunnies and teddies, or loaded (improbably) on to toy trains and space rockets! . . . extravagant – expensive – exciting! – which shall we choose?

A consumer magazine would tell us, no doubt, that there is more value for money in an ordinary bar of chocolate, weight for weight. Perhaps it depends on what you mean by value! There might be as much nourishment in a plate of rice pudding as in a dish of strawberries and cream, but we all know which we would probably choose. The scientists may invent an all-purpose food pill, but it will need a lot of work to persuade us to substitute it for our Sunday lunch!

The truth is that we need food for our imagination as well as for our bodies if we are to grow into whole peoples. What is more, our God who made us knows that we have need of these things too, and he has created a world that not only provides for our physical but also our spiritual needs.

The dancing daffodils that light up the world with their springtime radiance and the new buds on every wakening tree assure us that God not only gives us life, but makes it beautiful too. This is the bonus which the scientist and the technician can never provide. Ours is not just a functional world which is self-perpetuating and soulless, but a world where the spirit can grow in the sunlight of God's love.

So let the children have their Easter eggs and help them to see the symbolism in their chocolate treat: the promise of new life not only in the world of nature but in our hearts and minds.

It's just a thought . . .

READING

James 1:17-18

Every generous act of giving, with every perfect gift, is from above, coming down from the Father of lights, with whom there is no variation or shadow due to change. In fulfilment of his own purpose he gave us birth by the word of truth, so that we would become a kind of first fruits of his creatures.

PRAYER

God, you are the illuminator of our universe. You have filled our world with light and colour, fragrance and beauty, to uplift our souls. As we give you thanks for the new life around us, grant that we may be filled with new life within.

61

The maypole dance

'Hold on to your ribbons – *right* then left – *in* then out – no, no Samantha, *under,* not over! Stop – stop the music.'

The rehearsal staggered to an untidy finish. 'It's coming along, children,' Miss Lightfoot exclaimed encouragingly. 'We'll try again tomorrow!'

I had visions of that poor lady securely lashed to the maypole by her enthusiastic pupils! As I extricated my young daughter from the madding crowd I thought, 'Life is rather like a maypole dance.'

Here we are, skipping to the music, trying hard to get it right: some, energetic and purposeful, pursuing their course regardless of those coming in the opposite direction: some hesitant and dithery, unsure which way to go. The plodders with their heavy feet, a little puffed, not quite in time to the music. The perfectionists, pointing their toes, and going their own sweet way. The exhibitionists, showing off and getting it wrong. What a mess we make of it!

Our ribbons are many colours. What a dull pattern it would be if we were all the same. We must each hold on to our own ribbon and not let go; it is the symbol of our individualism. But we must co-operate with the other dancers if we are to create a pattern of balance and beauty. A maypole dance cannot be a solo performance!

So what is the secret of success?

One thing is certain – we need a maypole which is firmly anchored to the floor – one which will not topple over as it is pulled in different directions – a secure foundation on which to centre the dance. In our lives God provides that foundation. His love will not change or fail us no matter how many mistakes we make. And if we listen to the music, which is the essence of the dance, God, the great choreographer, has promised to guide our steps.

From where we dancers stand it is impossible to see the pattern we are weaving. It is only when the dance is over that we will be able to stand back and see the purpose of all our manoeuvres, and if we have interpreted it rightly we should have the satisfaction of having helped to complete a design, and the joy of having taken part.

It's just a thought . . .

READING

Psalm 149:3-4

Let them praise his name with dancing,
    making melody to him with tambourine and lyre.
For the LORD takes pleasure in his people;
    he adorns the humble with victory.

PRAYER

Lord of the dance, we thank you for inviting us to participate. Weave our steps into your pattern and let our performance be full of your grace.

62

Mayflowers

I was nearly a Mayflower once . . . but I got the mumps!

Our school held a special celebration every May Day. A Queen was chosen and the Caller of the Flowers summoned forth a bright and beautiful bunch of violets, rosebuds and mayflowers to dance before her.

Enraptured with my part, I practised assiduously – until the morning when I woke up with a sore throat and a face like a balloon! I stood at the window waving my friends off to school, my eyes brimming with tears caused not by the pain in my neck, but by the pain in my heart! A Mayflower with mumps! Inevitably someone took my place.

However, my story had an unexpectedly happy ending. I returned to school just before the Great Day, sadly resigned to a spectator's role, only to find that one of the Daisies had fallen by the wayside, and at short notice I was given a white dress, a wand and a crash course as *Bellis perennis*!

Life's disappointments are not all resolved as simply as that! Not all thwarted Mayflowers become Daisies, but if we trust him, God can make all things work together for good.

The anguish felt by the disciples on Good Friday was such that even the joy of Easter Day could not fully overcome it. Bewildered and lost, they were without heart for the present and without hope for the future. Then at Pentecost the Holy Spirit came, filling their lives with a power and purpose of which they had scarcely dreamed.

When events and disappointments have had their way, God sometimes surprises us!

It's just a thought . . .

READING

Romans 5:1-5

Therefore, since we are justified by faith, we have peace with God through our Lord Jesus Christ, through whom we have obtained access to this grace in which we stand; and we boast in our hope of sharing the glory of God. And not only that, but we also boast in our sufferings, knowing that suffering produces endurance, and endurance produces character, and character produces hope, and hope does not disappoint us, because God's love has been poured into our hearts through the Holy Spirit that has been given to us.

PRAYER

God of love, we cannot doubt that you want the best for your children. When we are frustrated in our plans, or when things do not work out the way we want them, help us to overcome our disappointment in the sure knowledge that all things work together for good for those who love you.

63

Points of view

The sun was shining on golden meadows, trees in new leaf, wild flowers in the hedgerows and the sparkling blue sea. The Devon countryside was full of springtime beauty and, in a field high on the hillside, a herd of black and white cows munched contentedly in the lush green grass. 'I wonder if they appreciate the view?' I thought.

Artistic cows? It's an interesting idea! Do cows look around them when they wander? How far can they see? Have they any sense of wonder, or are their sights limited to the quantity and quality of the grass at their feet?

It's so easy for *us* to become limited in our vision so that we see only the dust on the mantelpiece, the files in the 'In Tray' or the weeds in the garden path. Fortunately we *do* have the power of appreciation. There is a God-given spark within us which can respond to the beauty of sight and sound. But sometimes we let the spots on the windscreen obscure our view of the road ahead.

One of the first astronauts, heading for the moon, looked back on the earth, silently spinning in space with the light of the sun upon it and told how deeply he was moved by its cloud-swathed beauty, seeing it as a small vulnerable whole. All the unrest and disharmony of its continents – war, famine, poverty and disease – were made insignificant in the context of the universe.

Is this how God sees our world?

Jesus told us that the very hairs of our head are all numbered. Each one of us is precious in his sight, but in case we get 'bogged down' by the business of living he lifts our eyes to the horizon and shows us a still more glorious view.

It's just a thought . . .

READING

Psalm 121:1, 2, 5-8

I lift up my eyes to the hills –
    from where will my help come?
My help comes from the LORD,
    who made heaven and earth.

The LORD is your keeper;
    the LORD is your shade at your right hand.
The sun shall not strike you by day,
    nor the moon by night.

The LORD will keep you from all evil;
    he will keep your life.
The LORD will keep your going out and your coming in
    from this time on and forevermore.

PRAYER

God, our sun and our shield, lift our eyes towards you, we pray. As we worship you and give thanks for the beauty of your universe, help us to see beyond our limited horizons to a wider view of your glorious kingdom.

64

The energy gap

Do you find it difficult to get up in the mornings? Do you 'droop' in the middle of the day? Do you 'collapse' when you get home from work? Do you fall asleep in front of the television? Maybe you are deficient in iron or vitamins? Maybe you've outgrown your strength – or outworn your usefulness!

Maybe it's the energy gap!

Glancing through a pile of old magazines in the dentist's waiting-room it's possible to discover cures for all ills. You can bridge that gap with Somebody's Snack, or get a little lift from a well-known fizzy drink! There are 'pink pills for pale people' and 'sunshine supplements' for every age. When our energy flags we can combat fatigue and restore our zest for life with something sprinkled on our breakfast cereal or stirred into our bedtime drink!

But what about when our spiritual energy flags? When we feel disillusioned with the society in which we live – when we feel that the struggle is too uphill or the fight seems futile? When defeatism takes over and we find ourselves sinking into apathy and despair? The chemist and the health shop cannot help us then.

The message of Pentecost is sometimes difficult to understand. The imagery of rushing wind, of flames and tongues is something we cannot readily associate with everyday life. I think we feel that the coming of the Holy Spirit is something that only happens to special people in special circumstances. But if we can think of Pentecost as the tremendous energy of God coming into our lives, to fortify us and enable us to achieve all that he has promised us, we may even surprise ourselves with the results.

It's just a thought . . .

READING

Acts 2:1-4

When the day of Pentecost had come, they were all together in one place. And suddenly from heaven there came a sound like the rush of a violent wind, and it filled the entire house where they were sitting. Divided tongues, as of fire, appeared among them, and a tongue rested on each of them. All of them were filled with the Holy Spirit and began to speak in other languages, as the Spirit gave them ability.

PRAYER

God, great source of energy and power, refresh and revitalise us. When our spirits flag, when we get tired of trying, surprise us with your enabling Spirit and help us once more to get up and go.

65

Is there anybody there?

I dialled a number, heard the ringing tone, prepared myself to speak, and then came the impersonal voice which told me, 'This is a recorded message . . . please leave your name and number with details of your enquiry and your call will be returned as soon as possible.' Suddenly I was speechless!

There is something very daunting about talking to a machine. How can one explain a problem to a piece of electrical equipment? Without the comforting response of a friendly voice on the receiving end to prompt you into giving the right information, to reassure you that someone is listening to what you have to say, to let you know that your problem is understood, and to advise you what to do next, it is like sending a message into outer space!

Whereas the telephone can bring you into direct contact with another human being, the answerphone undermines your confidence – even makes you feel ridiculous – in sending words along the wires in the hope that someone will take note of them, and that what you have said will make sense. It's a bit like sending a message in a bottle across the sea! Who knows where it will land and who will find it?

Some people feel that way about prayer. Is anybody listening? Can anybody hear? Will anybody answer us? Many people will tell you, 'I do say my prayers, but I never get an answer.' Does God say, 'Leave your name and number and I will get in touch on my return'?

Perhaps this is the most meaningful message of Pentecost – not that God has installed an answerphone in heaven, but that through the coming of his Holy Spirit into the world he has given us a direct line. We have only to think about him to have him at our side or in our hearts and minds, listening to us, reassuring us, and guiding us in every moment of our lives.

It's just a thought . . .

READING

1 John 5:14-15

And this is the boldness we have in him, that if we ask anything according to his will, he hears us. And if we know that he hears us in whatever we ask, we know that we have obtained the requests made of him.

PRAYER

It's good to talk to you, Lord. We thank you for direct dialling. We thank you that the lines are never too busy for us to get through to you and we thank you that you are always ready to answer our call.

66

The power and the glory

Electricity bills are for most of us among the least welcome items of post. How interesting it was to learn, therefore, that one of our young student friends from Oxford was making a special study of solar energy.

One of the problems in this country is finding sufficient sunshine to promote experiments. It is obviously much easier to set up projects of this kind under the sunny skies of California, for instance, than under the umbrella of yesterday's weather forecast! But now it seems that scientists are making progress in using ordinary daylight to produce the energy which will supplement our heating systems and conserve the more traditional sources of fuel. Certainly it makes sense to use this wonderful natural source of power which is all around us.

Perhaps we may learn something here which can help us in our spiritual life too. Sometimes we may wish that we could have an experience such as the disciples had at Pentecost when flames of fire rested on their heads. We may envy the shepherds when they saw a 'great light' and 'glory shone around'. How easy it would be for us then to kindle a flame of sacred love in our hearts!

What we have to remember is that God sends his daylight into the world every day – a miracle as wonderful as any special revelation. The energy of his love and power is round about us all the time, even when it is obscured by clouds. It only waits for us to discover it and harness it to warm our hearts and the lives of those around us.

It's just a thought . . .

READING

Ephesians 3:20-21

Now to him who by the power at work within us is able to accomplish abundantly far more than all we can ask or imagine, to him be glory in the church and in Christ Jesus to all generations, forever and ever. Amen.

PRAYER

Most glorious God, creator of the sun which shines upon us, and of the clouds which overshadow us, help us to harness the power of your mighty Spirit to bring light and warmth into the dark cold places of our world.

67

Balloons

Where's the party? Follow the balloons! It has become a custom wherever there is a celebration to indicate the venue with bunches of balloons. Bright and beautiful, the gleaming globes bobbing in the breeze beckon us on to where the fun begins. The silent hullabaloo of balloons arouses in us an expectation of happiness. Whether it be the red balloon of childhood dreams tugging at the string on a baby's pram, a balloon in a box to say 'Happy Anniversary', or the release of a thousand shining spheres to mark a festival of joy, balloons will lift our eyes and our spirits to the skies.

There is something ethereal about a balloon but sadly it can be all too ephemeral as well. Hold tightly on to the string or the laughter turns to tears; make contact with a prickle and delight turns to dismay!

Sometimes our hopes and aspirations are like balloons. Lighter than air they fly to the heights but quickly let us down. Beware of thorns which lie waiting to deflate them. Hold on to the dream or it will disappear, leaving only a withered scrap of plastic which can never be repaired. But when the Holy Spirit fills our hearts it lifts them up, not like the gas in a balloon which soon expires, but like the breath of God inspiring us to make the dream come true.

Resistant to all life's pains and punctures, we can rise above them, and even when we let go of the string, we know that God will still be holding on to us.

It's just a thought . . .

READING

Psalm 108:3-5

I will give thanks to you, O Lord, among the peoples,
and I will sing praises to you among the nations.
For your steadfast love is higher than the heavens,
and your faithfulness reaches to the clouds.
Be exalted, O God, above the heavens,
and let your glory be over all the earth.

PRAYER

Breath of God, inspire our hearts so that we may rise above the things of the earth. Release us from the ties which pull us down, and let our spirits fly free within the confines of your love.

68

Wind of change

Isn't it maddening when you've just got a seat on the train at last, stowed your bags on the luggage rack, and settled down to read the paper when the guard calls out, 'All change here!' Have you noticed the air of disbelief among fellow travellers – trying to persuade themselves that they must have misheard the instructions? Then, as you file miserably on to the platform to wait for who-knows-what, there is always a reluctant passenger who sits tight in her seat in a vain attempt to make British Rail relent and take her where she wants to go!

I suppose we are all a little wary of change. Moving house, changing jobs, or even going on holiday are listed among the most stressful events in our lives. Even changing our hairstyle can cause panic as the scissors actually begin their devastating work!

'A change is as good as a rest,' we glibly say, but a change in our lifestyle can be anything but restful!

Nevertheless we all need change – without it we cannot grow. We do not know how a caterpillar feels when it spins a cocoon, but when it emerges as a butterfly we can see that the transformation has wonderful consequences.

Turning the corner the other day I was caught in a great gust of wind which nearly blew me over. Unseen and all-powerful, that great breath of fresh air made me think of the imagery of Pentecost when, like a great wind, the Holy Spirit invaded the hearts of the disciples, banishing fears and doubts and filling them with power and purpose – a wind of change which altered the course of their lives and, ultimately, of ours!

'All change' can be uncomfortable but the consequences can be miraculous.

It's just a thought . . .

READING

2 Corinthians 5:17

So if anyone is in Christ, there is a new creation: everything old has passed away: see, everything has become new.

PRAYER

Changeless God, we are afraid of the unknown. We, who are creatures of habit, do not like to be unsettled. When our lives are changed we feel insecure. Help us to realise that without change we cannot grow. Help us to know that whatever happens you are with us and your transforming love will never let us go.

69

Busting out!

'June is busting out all over!' – well, almost. Spring was a little retarded this year. Our tortoise, having emerged from hibernation at the end of April, took one look around and retreated into her shell again to shelter from the cold winds of May. The late frosts delayed the planting out of seedlings, and azalea buds which were poised tantalisingly ready to open, remained in a state of suspended animation until the warmth of the sun persuaded them to blossom forth. Perhaps we might say June was *creeping* out all over!

So what about us? As we rummage through the wardrobe to rediscover summer clothes, *busting out* might well be appropriate. Long winter evenings spent curled up in front of the television with 'comfort' nibbles of chocolate and crisps have probably done little to get us in trim. There they hang – the barely-worns, the misfits, the mistakes and the old faithfuls of former years, accusing us of wilful neglect. We hastily close the door and plan to start the diet – tomorrow.

After the amazing experience of Pentecost, Jesus' disciples were certainly busting out all over! Fired with enthusiasm for sharing the good news, they faced the dangers and challenges of their day with new confidence and joy. No-one could be in any doubt of their assurance.

By contrast, we are often more reticent in our witness. For many of us, it does not come easily to express exuberance in our worship or our work. Not being extrovert by nature, we are often wary of those who are. But the Holy Spirit works in many ways. A sparkle in someone's eye, an infectious smile, the warmth of a handshake or embrace, or the dependability of our friendship in times of trouble can speak as eloquently of God's love as many tongues.

Blessed by the Holy Spirit, the spring which is slow to start may blossom into the most glorious of summers.

It's just a thought . . .

READING

Acts 4:8-10 and 13

Then Peter, filled with the Holy Spirit, said to them, 'Rulers of the people and elders, if we are questioned today because of a good deed done to someone who was sick and are asked how this man has been healed, let it be known to all of you, and to all the people of Israel, that this man is standing before you in good health by the name of Jesus Christ of Nazareth, whom you crucified, whom God raised from the dead.'

Now when they saw the boldness of Peter and John and realised that they were uneducated and ordinary men, they were amazed and recognised them as companions of Jesus.

PRAYER

Holy Spirit, work through us, we pray, so that by the loving conduct of our lives we may be recognised as companions of Jesus.

70

Getting away from it all

Are you coming or going, I wonder? For months now, the thought of that holiday in the sun may have been spurring you on to make plans, to daydream a little, to save your money, to service the car, to indulge in an orgy of dressmaking! Visions of long lazy days on beaches or mountains, blue skies, delicious food, scintillating company; no restrictions, no pressure, no problems . . . getting away from it all.

Well, it may not have been *exactly* like that . . . there was that sand in the sandwiches, the blister on your heel, the queue that was *not* convenient! That couple at the next table who insisted on trying to make you laugh . . . the day it rained on the boat trip . . . the time when you lost the car keys . . . and wished, perhaps, that you were not quite so far away from it all.

What is it that we are all so anxious to get away from? Different things for different people, I suppose. Routine? Civilisation? Noise? Neighbours? The boss? Or just 'cooking the meals'?

Whatever it is, there invariably comes a time when, having *got* away from it all, we are quite glad to get *back* to it all again!

There is a lot to be said for the old routine, for the discomforts with which we are familiar, for the same predictable problems over which we sighed and seethed before! They make us feel that we belong, that we are needed.

So here's to holidays – long may they continue to relax and refresh us, to revive and restore us, and above all to remind us that life is where we are and that God is with us in every part of it.

It's just a thought . . .

READING

Psalm 139:7-10

Where can I go from your spirit?
    Or where can I flee from your presence?
If I ascend to heaven, you are there;
    if I make my bed in Sheol, you are there;
If I take the wings of the morning
    and settle at the farthest limits of the sea,
even there your hand shall lead me,
    and your right hand shall hold me fast.

PRAYER

Ever-present God, you know us better than we know ourselves. When we are restless and in need of change, or when we are trapped in a familiar routine, your caring presence still surrounds us. We thank you that wherever we go we cannot escape from your love.

71

Ice-cream Sunday

Holiday time is here – sun, sand and ice-cream sundaes. All over the country families will be enjoying the annual break from routine. We were on holiday when one of our daughters celebrated her fourth birthday so her party had to be deferred until we returned home. Instead we visited an Ice-Cream Parlour for a rare treat. Cones were run-of-the-mill. Even lollies lacked lustre, but the *pièce de résistance* – the Knickerbocker Glory – was a delight as yet untasted. The anticipation was exquisite and when the waitress arrived with the tall glasses on a tray, the birthday girl had to stand on her chair to get the long spoon into the glass!

My small grandson told me he takes sandwiches to school for lunch each day except Fridays when he has a hot dinner – 'the Friday Special' – which is usually fish and chips!

As Christians we have designated Sunday as *our* special day – but do we look forward to it and regard it as a treat? Washing the car, digging the garden, painting the ceiling, preparing Sunday lunch; entertaining visitors while trying to keep the family happy, rushing to get to church on time – all these things often mean that Sunday finds us distracted and tense and by the evening we are worn out rather than refreshed. I know sometimes I *scream*, 'Sunday again!'

We know that God is with us all the week, but perhaps we undervalue our Special Day. It is so easy to fill it with chores and duties, making burdens for ourselves. Our seventh day was meant to be a time of happiness and blessing – a precious opportunity to be ourselves, to share with one another, and to feel the power and love of God touching our lives, giving us strength for all that lies ahead in our busy week. When all is said and done there really *is* something to be said for Keeping Sunday Special!

It's just a thought . . .

READING

Exodus 23:12-13

Six days you shall do your work, but on the seventh day you shall rest; so that your ox and your donkey may have relief, and your homeborn slave . . . may be refreshed.

PRAYER

Lord of the sabbath, we thank you for our Special Day. Help us to delight in it, and, not bound by rules and regulations but only by the law of love, to use each precious moment for each other and for you.

72

Travelling light

Off on holiday? How do you pack your case? Are you a 'layer-in-tissue-paper' packer? – or one of the 'roll-up-and-stuff' brigade?

At Waterloo station some years ago *en route* for our annual Brownie pack holiday, the bottom fell out of somebody's carrier bag, depositing trainers, toothbrush, sandwiches and sundry items of underwear on the line between platform and train! Fortunately a resourceful porter retrieved them with a sort of fishing rod!

On another occasion, some friends returning from a caravan holiday opened their cases to reveal a clothes line complete with the washing still pegged on it!

But whether you are the kind of person who requires a trunk for a weekend break, or a plastic bag for a trip round the world – packing is an art.

Life is often likened to a journey and here, too, many of us have trouble with our luggage. We lumber ourselves with extraneous paraphernalia and make heavy weather of the going because we are overloaded with goods and cares, habits, commitments and trivialities. We set out struggling with our cases and forget that we have left our tickets on the mantelpiece!

When Jesus sent out his twelve disciples he briefed them, 'Take nothing for your journey – neither a stick, nor a purse, nor food, nor money – not even extra clothes.' All we really need is a survival kit!

So when we are cramming in the suntan lotion with the wellington boots, we should spare a thought for the rest of our encumbrances – are we struggling through life with unnecessary burdens? And what would we have to show for it if the bottom fell out of *our* carrier bag?

It's just a thought . . .

READING

Matthew 11:28-30

Come to me, all you that are weary and are carrying heavy burdens, and I will give you rest. Take my yoke upon you, and learn from me; for I am gentle and humble in heart, and you will find rest for your souls. For my yoke is easy, and my burden is light.

PRAYER

Jesus, our travelling companion, as we continue on life's journey, help us to know what to take; so that when we arrive at your kingdom and unpack our luggage before you, we may not feel ashamed.

73

Footprints in the sand

One of the nicest things about the seaside is walking barefoot on the sands. Making the very first footprints on an untrodden beach is perhaps the most delightful of all.

The morning sun was glinting on the wide wet sands when we set out to walk along the beautiful Pembrokeshire coastal path, but we were not the first to walk that way. Ahead of us was a trail of footprints criss-crossing the beach, telling their story of the ones who had gone before.

Trainers with their tyre-like tread zigzagged across the strand mingled with the imprint of fishermen's boots, stiletto heels and the myriad patterns of sandals and shoes scurrying all around. We followed a pair of little 'barefoot' prints right down to the water's edge where they suddenly turned and fled back again to the safety of the shore! There were hop, skip and jump prints where the world had passed by, churning up the beach with the activities of the day – building castles, making pies, digging holes, dragging deck-chairs and baskets and boats through the dunes, all leaving their marks behind. One thing was reassuring – the next tide would soon roll in to erase all that turmoil and restore the beach to its golden glory, washed smooth, clean and perfect as God had created it.

A bit like our day, which starts fresh and new, untrodden and perfect until we get out of bed and put our foot in it! However determined we are to be positive, loving and kind, it will not be long before we have made our first blunder – banged on the bathroom door, complained at the burnt toast, moaned over a large bill, or fumed over a late train.

Not many of us will commit a criminal offence, but all of us will leave scuff marks in the sand. What a blessing that the tide of God's love comes in to wash away the mistakes we have made and give us a clean start tomorrow!

It's just a thought . . .

READING

Micah 7:18-19
Who is a God like you, pardoning iniquity
and passing over the transgression
of the remnant of your possession?
He does not retain his anger forever,
because he delights in showing clemency.
He will again have compassion upon us;
He will tread our iniquities under foot.
You will cast all our sins into
the depths of the sea.

PRAYER

Forgiving God, we thank you for your endless patience with us. Our best intentions so often go astray. When our footsteps wander, when we spoil your world by our neglect or wilfulness, when relationships break down, help us to admit our faults and in true repentance turn to you. Grant us forgiveness and the chance to start again.

74

Sit-uation

What you see depends a great deal upon where you sit. I suppose that many of us will have suffered at some time from viewing the play from a seat behind a lady's large hat!

The most extraordinary vantage point I have ever seen was on a visit to Eastbourne. It was a glorious summer's day, the promenade was festooned with row upon row of blue and white deck-chairs, and crowds sat in the sunshine, drinking in the beauty of the sparkling scene. Then we came across a group of determined picnickers sitting not on the beach or the grassy slopes, not in the flower-filled gardens brilliant with colour, not on the cliff-side paths, the rockeries or sand-dunes – but in the gloom and cold *under the pier*! All they could see was a conglomeration of rusty iron girders and the accumulated rubbish of empty tins and fish and chip papers, orange peel and lolly sticks, trapped by the tide and floating in the scummy water. It had to be seen to be believed!

We cannot always choose where we sit. Sometimes our seats are chosen for us. Certainly our impression of life will be coloured by our sit-uation.

Sometimes we need to sit down beside the suffering and sorrowful in order to understand and comfort them.

Jesus was much criticised by the 'religious' people of his day for sitting down to eat with 'tax collectors and sinners'. It was only by seeing the world through their eyes that he could show them his love and care.

It is important for us to stand up for our beliefs – dare I say that we must also be prepared to sit down with those around us and see what they see too?

It's just a thought . . .

READING

Luke 5:27-32

After this he went out and saw a tax collector named Levi, sitting at the tax booth; and he said to him, 'Follow me.' And he got up, left everything and followed him.

Then Levi gave a great banquet for him in his house; and there was a large crowd of tax collectors and others sitting at the table with them. The Pharisees and their scribes were complaining to his disciples, saying, 'Why do you eat and drink with tax collectors and sinners?' Jesus answered, 'Those who are well have no need of a physician, but those who are sick; I have come to call not the righteous but sinners to repentance.'

PRAYER

God of understanding, help us to understand. Save us from arrogance and from judging others. Help us always to be ready to sit down beside those who need us, and to see what they see. Help us always to be ready to kneel down beside you and see what you see.

75

Here today . . .

There was such excitement! The holiday chalet overlooked the sands and sea, and just a few yards along the sea-front in all its glittering glory was a FAIR! Our children were fascinated. Each evening as we walked along the promenade, we savoured the inviting sound of the hurdy-gurdy music, saw the prancing horses on the roundabout and watched the twinkling lights whirl high in the darkening sky.

Holiday pocket money would run to only one visit to the fair so we decided to save that for Friday, the last night of the holiday, to provide a memorable climax to the week. On Friday morning we woke early, eager not to miss a moment of that special day. Then, as we headed for the beach, we were suddenly stopped in our tracks by what we saw. Like a mirage in the desert, the fair had disappeared – packed up and gone in the night leaving no trace! To this day our daughters still recall their bitter disappointment. Other treats were offered – a Knickerbocker Glory, a late-night paddle in the sea – but nothing could compensate for that promised visit to the fair. We had left it too late.

We have all known the heartache of leaving it too late. When sudden disaster or pain touches our lives we all experience the pangs of regret for unfinished business – remorse for the hasty action, the unkind remark, or the unspoken word. I do not believe that God expects us to live our lives in anxiety about the future, measuring every word and action in anticipation of events beyond our control. We simply do what seems best from day to day, secure in the knowledge that his love bridges time and space. But there are some things that we can do here and now, like mending a quarrel, asking forgiveness, or telling someone we love them *today*.

It's just a thought . . .

READING

Matthew 4:18-22

As he walked by the Sea of Galilee, he saw two brothers, Simon, who is called Peter, and Andrew his brother, casting a net into the sea – for they were fishermen. And he said to them, 'Follow me, and I will make you fish for people.' Immediately they left their nets and followed him. As he went from there, he saw two other brothers, James son of Zebedee and his brother John, in the boat with their father Zebedee, mending their nets, and he called them. Immediately they left the boat and their father, and followed him.

PRAYER

God of the here and now, save us from procrastination. Forgive our feeble excuses for putting things off and give us a sense of urgency in doing your will. We cannot alter the past; neither can we know the future, but you have given us today in which to serve you. We thank you for the precious gift of *now*.

76

Keeping in touch

Here come the holiday postcards: 'Sunset over the Sahara', 'Llandudno by Night' or 'Two pebbles on the beach in Corfu'. We call it keeping in touch! True 'keeping in touch', however, involves much more than this. Christians are often accused of being 'out of touch' with reality, with little knowledge of or concern for the problems and needs of the community.

Keeping in touch means more than the occasional sortie into everyday life. It is all too easy for us to cut ourselves off by using obscure language or by paying lip service only to addressing the social problems of our day.

One of my daughters told me this delightful story. Teaching a class of eight-year-olds how the ear works, she explained how sound enters the ear and sets up vibrations on the eardrum which transmits a message to the brain. One little girl, having followed the progress of the sound this far, concluded her work by writing, '. . . and then it goes out of the *uvver* ear'! Truer perhaps than she realised.

Jesus was always in touch. He sat down to eat with tax collectors. He challenged the religious leaders; he touched the lepers. He went outside the synagogue to preach to people in their everyday language. His parables were about things which concerned them: catching fish, market-place transactions, looking after sheep. If he were here today he would surely have something to say to the accountant, the computer programmer, the mechanic or sales assistant, and be able to relate to the problems of homelessness, poverty and discrimination.

To keep in touch means not just hearing or even understanding the needs of others, but so practising the presence of God that his love will motivate and influence our actions too.

It's just a thought . . .

READING

Matthew 25:34-40

Then the king will say to those at his right hand, 'Come, you that are blessed by my Father, inherit the kingdom prepared for you from the foundation of the world; for I was hungry and you gave me food, I was thirsty and you gave me something to drink, I was a stranger and you welcomed me, I was naked and you gave me clothing, I was sick and you took care of me, I was in prison and you visited me.' Then the righteous will answer him, 'Lord, when was it that we saw you hungry and gave you food, or thirsty and gave you something to drink? And when was it that we saw you a stranger and welcomed you, or naked and gave you clothing? And when was it that we saw you sick or in prison and visited you?' And the king will answer them, 'Truly I tell you, just as you did it to one of the least of these who are members of my family, you did it to me.'

PRAYER

Jesus, touchstone of our love, keep us always in touch with you and with the needs of the world around us today.

77

Anything to declare?

For most of us the trip through Customs on return from our holiday abroad simply adds to the excitement of travel to foreign parts. It encourages the spirit of adventure and we feel almost disappointed when we are happily waved through without a search of our cases, even though we have nothing more sinister to hide than a bag of dirty socks! Even so, we may well have a slightly guilty feeling when joining the 'Nothing to Declare' queue. Perhaps we feel we *should* have something to declare!

Notices warn us 'NEVER be tempted to smuggle'. What tell-tale signs do Customs Officers look for as they scrutinise the line of passengers filing past them with 'nothing to declare'? It's probably a professional secret but we assume they are looking for signs of nervousness. Anyone talking loudly or seeming to be in a hurry is therefore a likely candidate for a spot check!

The Bible spells it out too! 'The heavens declare the glory of God' we read. But have we anything to declare? When we leave church on Sunday and resume our journey through the week, are we prepared for the spot check? When confronted with a problem at work, do we display signs of nervousness – following the crowd and hoping no-one will notice? When we chat with our neighbours at the shops, do we talk loudly about the state of the world but hurry past the next collecting box? When we hear unkind gossip or racist comment, do we let it pass unchallenged?

Are we sometimes tempted to smuggle our good intentions through without declaring them and without acting upon them? Followers of Jesus must always have something to declare. To declare ourselves is to avow our intentions – to disclose our character or attitude – not just in words but in the way we live our lives.

It's just a thought . . .

READING

1 Chronicles 16:23-25

Sing to the Lord, all the earth.
Tell of his salvation from day to day.
Declare his glory among the nations,
his marvellous works among all the peoples.
For great is the Lord, and greatly to be praised;
he is to be revered above all gods.

PRAYER

All-seeing God, you know what is in our hearts. Give us the courage to declare our beliefs, the boldness to stand up for what we know to be true, and the gallantry to dare all things for you.

78

Growing up

'My! Haven't you grown!' is something we all say when young children come to visit. The wonder would be if they *hadn't* grown, and yet we still find it a never-ending source of astonishment.

During the last week of the school holidays, the shoe shops are crowded with parents having their children's feet measured for the next size up before they return to school. For four or five-year-olds, it is a source of pride to be told how big they are. Later in life, it is probably something we would rather have left unsaid!

Most of us stop growing when in our late teens, after which we certainly do not wish anyone to comment on our size.

Scientists tell us our capacity for learning reaches its peak at around thirty years of age – so what shall we do with the rest of our lives?

Fortunately our difficulty in grasping new concepts should be compensated for by experience and, hopefully, wisdom. The trouble is that with physical and mental maturity, we sometimes cease to grow spiritually. With age it is all too easy for our attitudes to harden and for us to bring the same reactions to bear on life's challenges as we did when we were children – wanting our own way, failing to share, fostering petty grievances and looking inwards rather than out.

God gives us, his children, a span of years in which to learn and develop. Throughout our lives he wants us to grow in love and understanding, to stretch ourselves and realise our full potential.

When we reach our *harvest home*, wouldn't it be great to hear him say, 'How you have grown!'

It's just a thought . . .

READING

1 Corinthians 13:10-12

But when the complete comes, the partial will come to an end. When I was a child, I spoke like a child, I thought like a child, I reasoned like a child; when I became an adult, I put an end to childish ways. For now we see in a mirror, dimly, but then we will see face to face. Now I know only in part; then I will know fully, even as I have been fully known.

PRAYER

God of the harvest, help us to keep on growing. You alone know our full potential; you value each one of us throughout our lives. Help us not to become stunted or self-satisfied, but to develop in the light of your encouragement until we are the people you want us to be.

79

Putting the clocks back

Everyone knows that you can't 'put the clock back', and yet once a year we do just that!

With the ending of Summer Time, we all have the chance to do what we so often wish for – to 'relive' a little bit of our lives!

If we altered the clock before we went to bed on Saturday then maybe we had that precious hour between nine and ten or ten and eleven to live again! What did *you* do with this unique opportunity, I wonder?

Did you read a really worthwhile book that you have never had time for before? Did you paint a picture, or write a letter, or compose a song?

My guess is that most of us said, 'Ah – an extra hour in bed tomorrow', and probably, as I did, slept on a little later and never even realised the chance we had been given!

Of course it's all hypothetical really. Whatever pranks we may play with the hands of the clock we cannot really alter time. For 'time' is only a human device. God's world is a timeless one, and because we cannot go back into the past, or see into the future, the only real 'time' we have is the present moment. What matters is not what we did yesterday or what we intend doing tomorrow, but what we are doing right now at this moment.

I believe that God intends us to live every day to the full, and that it is the quality of our lives, not the length of our days, which makes our small contribution to eternal life.

So when we are next tempted to say, 'If I could have my time over again . . .' perhaps we should say instead, '*Today* I am going to really live.'

It's just a thought . . .

READING

2 Corinthians 6:1-2

As we work together with him, we urge you also not to accept the grace of God in vain. For he says,
　'At an acceptable time I have listened to you,
　and on a day of salvation I have helped you.'
See, now is the acceptable time; see, now is the day of salvation!

PRAYER

Time-keeper divine, we ask you to bless us today. Help us to live each moment of it – not looking back but looking up to you.

80

Vive la différence!

I stood beside the new photocopier, pressed the appropriate buttons, and miraculously it produced fifteen copies in as many seconds – every one identical! Just one of the wonders of technology which we take for granted today.

I stood in front of the tinned soup department in the superstore. There, fifty-seven varieties in standard tins were stacked in uniformed rows. We visited a Midlands city to shop, and found M&S, BHS, C&A and Mothercare – all just like home!

We walked along the seashore on a summer's day. A million pebbles glistened in the sun; no two were exactly alike, although we searched and searched. We took the Tube and underground the crowds milled past but no two faces were the same; just one of the miracles of God's creation.

This world is full of such rich diversity that we can scarcely take it in – and yet we spend a lot of our time striving for conformity and trying to persuade others to do things our way. Being united does not mean being uniform! Just as children in a family often differ from one another not only in looks but in personality, so surely there is room in God's family for all of us.

We shall soon be celebrating our Harvest Festival and as we look around at the abundance of colour, shape, texture and smell that we find in creation, let's rejoice that God, who made one hundred thousand species of butterflies alone, didn't use a photocopier when he made us, and give thanks that we all have a unique contribution to make.

'I just thank you, Father, for making me *me*.'

It's just a thought . . .

READING

Romans 12:4-8

For as in one body we have many members, and not all the members have the same function, so we, who are many, are one body in Christ, and individually we are members one of another. We have gifts that differ according to the grace given to us: prophecy, in proportion to faith; ministry, in ministering; the teacher, in teaching; the exhorter, in exhortation; the giver, in generosity; the leader, in diligence; the compassionate, in cheerfulness.

PRAYER

Wonderful God, you have made a multicoloured, multifarious world. We marvel at the variety of your creation. Most of all we thank you for making us each different from the other. We offer our diverse gifts to you.

81

Safely gathered in

As autumn comes a great many strange little creatures may be seen scurrying around indoors. There is a friendly spider who appears to live behind our television, and who often dashes out across the carpet during *News at Ten* – presumably to indulge his interest in current affairs – and then beats a hasty retreat before he can be returned to the great outdoors.

One or two weary wasps appear to have given up the struggle and collapsed behind the curtains, and it is not so long ago that daddy-long-legs insisted on coming in every time the front door was opened after dark! A short exploration of the garden shed reveals a conglomeration of small sleepy beetles, while a brave little woodlouse marches determinedly from under some flowerpots to fresh pastures.

Sensing that winter is on the way, these small friends of the earth are seeking shelter from the hardships ahead. How like us they are! Carefree and careless in the balmy days of summer, we take the whole world in our stride; but when life gets tough and difficulties face us, we scurry home to God, sometimes to question and to blame, sometimes to seek solace and strength, but always to find shelter in his loving care.

There are many in our community, however, who do not have that resource. When winter comes in its many forms, they do not know where to find consolation. At our Harvest Festival we will probably have sung our praises, offered thanks and revelled in the warm glow of a Harvest Home. If we can find ways to share that comfort and shelter with those in need, all may indeed be 'safely gathered in'.

It's just a thought . . .

READING

Isaiah 25:1 and 4

O Lord, you are my God;
I will exalt you, I will praise your name;
for you have done wonderful things,
plans formed of old, faithful and sure.

For you have been a refuge to the poor,
a refuge to the needy in their distress,
a shelter from the rainstorm and a shade from the heat.

PRAYER

God our refuge, when troubles come and we have nowhere else to go, we turn to you. We thank you that nothing can separate us from your love. Help us to share that love with those who have no shelter from life's storms and bring us all safely home.

82

Accident or design?

Do you know your Renoir from your Rembrandt? Can you recognise a Monet or a Michelangelo? Or distinguish Poynter from Picasso? Each artist has an inimitable style – the master's touch.

On a lower plane, perhaps, you may be able to identify a 'Laura Ashley' or a 'Liberty' design. Even the chain stores have adopted an image which is distinctly their own.

As we celebrate our Harvest Festival and give thanks for the fruits of the earth we are reminded again of its beauty. Colour, shape and fragrance combine to bring us not only sustenance for the body but delight for the senses.

On holiday we stood on Dartmoor and drank in the splendour of that superb landscape. What artist could have designed a canvas so perfect?

When we look at clouds in the sky we can see patterns which are recreated in waves on the shore. The delicate tracery of leaves is mirrored in feathers and shells. Colours of flowers appear again in rainbows and butterfly wings – a perfection created by a Mastermind.

If we ever have doubts about Creation – was it just an accident after all? – we have only to look around us to recognise the Master's touch. God's signature is upon the world as surely as an artist signs his work or a chain store sews in its label.

Can we doubt that we too are part of that design?

It's just a thought . . .

READING

Proverbs 8:27-31

When he established the heavens, I was there,
    when he drew a circle on the face of the deep,
when he made firm the skies above,
    when he established the fountains of the deep,
when he assigned to the sea its limit,
    so that the waters might not transgress his command,
when he marked out the foundations of the earth,
then I was beside him, like a master worker;
and I was daily his delight, rejoicing before him always,
rejoicing in his inhabited world and delighting in the human race.

PRAYER

Architect divine, we look in wonder on the beauty of your creation. With all our human skills of art and science we cannot conceive a design so immense and yet so intricate. We are humbled when confronted with the glory of your universe and give you thanks that we, too, have a place in your great plan.

83

Supporting cast

October is here – the golden month when leaves crackle like cornflakes underfoot, when late sunshine glimmers through the branches and the blue smoke of the bonfires wafts across gardens in the afternoon. Time to put the kettle on, make toast for tea and draw the curtains early. The holidays are over and memories of sea and sand are fading – but hurrah! – the holiday photos have arrived and we can recapture those halcyon days once more.

'That's a splendid view of the bay – pity it was so misty – look, there's our Linda, just behind the litter bin!' 'Oh, that *is* a good snap of Aunty Gladys – is that a flagpole growing out of the top of her head?'

'And who are those people walking past?' *You* don't know, neither do I, but they appear in countless holiday photos: the deckchair attendants and the lifeguards; the ice-cream vendors; the people who sat at the next table. We don't know their names; we can't even remember their faces, but they were there – the 'extras' or 'supporting cast' who just by their presence contributed to the saga of our holiday. The boy who clipped our tickets, the girl who served our tea, the kids who knocked our sandcastle over! And who knows, when they look at *their* holiday photos, perhaps we shall be there, members of the supporting cast in *their* star performance.

Who says we are independent? Our holiday snaps remind us that we are all involved with one another, even if we are just one of the crowd. And in God's greater plan we all have a part to play.

It's just a thought . . .

READING

Ecclesiastes 4:9-10

Two are better than one, because they have a good reward for their toil. For if they fall, one will lift up the other; but woe to one who is alone and falls and does not have another to help.

PRAYER

Loving God, you gave us one another to help us on our way. In the drama of life you have a part for us all. Whether we hold the stage or play a supporting role, help us to look to you for our direction.

84

What would you like for Christmas?

Did you ever visit Father Christmas? Did you ride on a magic sleigh, enter a fairy castle or walk through enchanted caves? Did you meet that white-bearded figure with his cheeks as red as his robes? Did you sit on his knee, I wonder, and look at his smiling face and whisper what you were longing to find in that pillowcase at the foot of your bed on Christmas Day? Did you ever wonder if he was real, half hoping that it might be so?

And what did you ask for, I wonder. Was it a bicycle or a doll? A puppy or a pair of skates? Or snow on Christmas Day?

Some of us may feel that we have grown too old for Father Christmas, but we still have wishes in our hearts. Perhaps this is why we endue God with flowing robes and a long white beard, while heaven becomes a magic cavern which we enter, a little fearfully, to whisper our requests in his ear. Sometimes we are disappointed and then we say he is not real. It is as though we have some sort of productivity deal with God.

Children are wonderfully optimistic – they ask for the moon at times! The trouble with most of us adults is that we don't ask God for enough! There are many of us who still only pray for that bicycle when we should be asking to be taught how to ride one.

So by all means let us hang up our Christmas stockings and let our requests be known, but in the sure knowledge that God is not just a kind of benevolent Santa Claus, but a loving Creator who longs to do for us far more than we ask or think.

It's just a thought . . .

READING

Matthew 7:7-8

Ask, and it will be given you; search, and you will find; knock, and the door will be opened for you. For everyone who asks receives, and everyone who searches finds, and for everyone who knocks, the door will be opened.

PRAYER

Almighty God, open our hearts to you and teach us to pray. We bring our requests to you only half-believing, and sometimes do not recognise the answers that you give. Your wise and loving care protects us from ourselves. Lord, we believe; help us to trust you more.

85

What shall we give them?

The great Christmas present season is here, and with it the vexed question, 'What do you give people who have everything?'

The catalogues are full of bright ideas – surely there is something here? An 'automatic cordless card shuffler' . . . or a 'motorised tie and belt selector' (complete with integral light for dark cupboards!) . . . or how about a set of 'wonder buttons' for too-tight clothes? However have we managed without them?

For the children it is easier. Bigger and better toys crowd us out, and the TV adverts will provide enough ideas for ten Christmases to come. Whatever happened to the original Christmas stocking with its little treats of sugar mice, chocolate money, peg dolls and an orange or a nut? But if the presents grow in size and expense it is the manufacturers who supply them and we adults who buy them who must take the blame. For it is a well-known fact that young children often prefer to play with the boxes the presents came in!

Perhaps the most precious gift we can give to anyone does not come in a box at all – the gift of our time and our love. Time to talk with and to read to our children and show them some of the wonders of God's world. Time to run about in the golden autumn leaves, to notice the design on a snowflake or the pattern of the clouds. Time to listen to our friends and to share their hopes and fears. Many would rather have a visit than the most elaborate present.

Wise men made a long journey to bring gifts to the Christ Child. That journey was part of the gift. God came to our world at

Christmas – not to send us his gifts but to bring them himself and to be with us for all time.

It's just a thought . . .

READING

Matthew 2:1-2 and 7-11

In the time of King Herod, after Jesus was born in Bethlehem in Judea, wise men from the East came to Jerusalem asking, 'Where is the child who has been born King of the Jews? For we observed his star at its rising, and have come to pay him homage.'

Then Herod secretly called for the wise men and learned from them the exact time when the star had appeared. Then he sent them to Bethlehem, saying, 'Go and search diligently for the child; and when you have found him, bring me word so that I may also go and pay him homage'. When they had heard the king, they set out; and there, ahead of them, went the star that they had seen at its rising, until it stopped over the place where the child was. When they saw that the star had stopped, they were overwhelmed with joy. On entering the house, they saw the child with Mary his mother; and they knelt down and paid him homage. Then, opening their treasure chests, they offered him gifts of gold, frankincense and myrrh.

PRAYER

Giver of all good gifts, guide our footsteps towards those who need us, and help us to share with them the gift of your love.

86

Window-shopping

The lights are twinkling amid garlands of ribbons; stars and baubles adorn the trees, and in the weeks before Christmas every shop window is a treasure chest of delight! A stroll down Regent Street becomes an exercise in art and design that whets our appetites for things beyond our reach. Of course, it is essential to do our window-shopping in the evenings so that we may feast our eyes on the lavishness of the unobtainable, safe in the knowledge that the shops are closed! But then, we're 'only looking'!

There are many parts of the world where window-shopping is the only kind. The riches of the western world compare starkly with the poverty of under-developed countries. Can they only look?

Sometimes we go 'window-shopping' in church! A stirring hymn, a moving prayer or an inspirational reading of God's word may give us a glimpse into a kingdom which is far removed from the troubled world around us. Suddenly we feel within reach of something wonderful – peace on earth and goodwill to all. We see a world where the hungry are fed, where children can grow up in love and security and where all things work together for good. Too expensive? This is a store where the merchandise is freely available – but the cost may be too much for us to pay. For to bring in God's kingdom we may have to give up many things – our preconceived notions and prejudices, our self-interests, maybe our time and talents. Too often the answer is 'we're only looking' – window-shopping when God waits to do for us more than we can ever ask or think.

It's just a thought . . .

READING

Luke 18:18-24

A certain ruler asked him, 'Good Teacher, what must I do to inherit eternal life? Jesus said to him, 'Why do you call me good? No one is good but God alone. You know the commandments: "You shall not commit adultery; You shall not murder; You shall not steal; You shall not bear false witness; Honour your father and mother."' He replied, 'I have kept all these since my youth.' When Jesus heard this, he said to him, 'There is still one thing lacking. Sell all that you own and distribute the money to the poor, and you will have treasure in heaven; then come, follow me.' But when he heard this, he became sad; for he was very rich. Jesus looked at him and said, 'How hard it is for those who have wealth to enter the kingdom of God!'

PRAYER

Good Teacher, your kingdom is inviting and we want to follow you, but often we are not prepared to pay the price. We look but we do not buy. Help us not just to stand outside and dream but spend ourselves and enter in.

87

Seeing stars

When was the last time you did some star-gazing, I wonder?

Perhaps, when you were a child, you enjoyed looking at the sky. Maybe your earliest conscious study of the stars was in camp or on board ship; or it may have been your first romance which set you gazing skywards. But I suspect that for many of us it may have been a long time since we really looked at the heavens other than briefly, through the bedroom curtains, or for those of us who sit up late enough to watch *The Sky at Night* on TV!

So button up your overcoat and come with me for a moment into the garden where I will show you something really great!

I know you are busy with your cake-making, tied up with paper chains, producing pantomimes, writing Christmas cards, and wondering how you will ever get through . . .

But pause, take a breath, look at the stars above you, and the bustle will seem irrelevant. Set against those sparkling symbols of eternity, how petty our problems appear!

And if the frenzy of Christmas has passed you by, maybe the festive season returns only to emphasise your feeling of isolation and loneliness. Then come and gaze at the sky for a moment, and look, and look again. The longer we look the more we shall see. A million star-worlds created by God who loves us all must surely guarantee that we are never really alone.

Maybe you feel doubtful and perplexed. But look above you and remember that those very stars were seen by the Wise Men in their far country. And, as the old year ends and a new year begins, may the Star of Christmas lead us on with hope and confidence to 'serve right gloriously, the God who gave all worlds that are, and all that are to be'.

It's just a thought . . .

READING

Psalm 8:3-5 and 9

When I look at your heavens, the work of your fingers,
    the moon and the stars that you have established;
what are human beings that you are mindful of them,
    mortals that you care for them?
Yet you have made them a little lower than God,
    and crowned them with glory and honour.
O LORD, our Sovereign,
    how majestic is your name in all the earth!

PRAYER

God of all brilliance, we gaze in awe at your creation. The heavens declare your glory and we worship you. You are our God and we are filled with wonder that you have made us partners in your mighty plan.

88

Labels

'Are you the Egg Mayonnaise?' The question still brings a smile to my lips after all these years. It was asked by a harassed waitress in a tearoom one Saturday afternoon when I had been shopping with a friend. 'No, we're the Toasted Teacakes!' we managed to reply before falling off our chairs in a fit of giggles.

We do tend to label people by outward appearances. Are you the Leopardskin Coat, or the Leather Jacket by any chance? Or, worse still, 'the Yuppie', 'the Lager Lout' or 'the Dropout'?

Putting labels on people can be a very dangerous practice. We constantly hear references to 'the Elderly', 'the Disabled' or 'the Unemployed'. It's so convenient to take great sections of the community and lump them all together under one heading. As though elderly people were not as varied and individual in their personalities and needs as they were in the days of their youth. Or as though sitting in a wheelchair or flaunting a different hairstyle automatically makes one a sinner or a saint!

It's nearly Christmas, and soon we will be doing battle with the tissue, the tinsel and the sellotape again. Whatever you do, get the labels right!

It's very disconcerting for Aunt Jemima to receive the aftershave while Uncle Bert gets the boudoir cap! But remember, it's even more disastrous for *people* to have the wrong label affixed to *them* – for the Shy to be labelled 'unfriendly', or for the Stranger to be labelled 'odd'.

Luckily for us, God doesn't have much use for labels – or that Babe might have been labelled 'Intentionally Homeless' and that Stable labelled 'Slum'!

It's just a thought . . .

READING

Romans 9:25-26

As indeed he says in Hosea,
> 'Those who were not my people I will call "my people",
> and her who was not beloved I will call "beloved".'
> 'And in the very place where it was said to them,
> "You are not my people",
> there they shall be called children of the living God.'

PRAYER

We are glad, God, that you do not categorise us, but that you value us as individuals. For you have created us to be our own person. You do not see us as the world sees us. You recognise our worth and our potential. Help us to be worthy of your high calling.

89

The real thing

There it stands – the fir tree – brought in from the cold, ready to be decorated. Tinsel, toys and treats will soon bedeck its branches, and on Christmas Day family and friends will gather round, faces smiling in the glow of the fairy lights. The tree – a focal point for the giving and goodwill that is Christmas.

Once we bought an artificial tree. It looked cheerful enough with its shining boughs and plastic berries. It certainly made less mess on the carpet! No pine needles dropping around, no need to water it, and when Christmas was over we folded it up and put it away in a box! But something was missing. There is no substitute for the real thing: a tree with bushy branches bringing its tangy fragrance into the room, a tree with roots, that we can plant in the garden when all the festivities are over, an evergreen symbol of life and growth.

Sometimes our celebration of Christmas is like that artificial tree. The glitter and the glamour is there, but no life. And when Christmas is over, back it goes in the box, leaving no trace.

Our expectation is that Christmas will be a time for togetherness, when all our petty grievances are laid aside for a few days and we will look kindly upon each other. It's Christmas – and we want everyone to be happy. Our compassion extends even beyond our own four walls to the wider family of God. We find ourselves reaching out to the lonely and isolated, the frail and the deprived, the hungry and the oppressed, bringing them into the family circle and touching their lives with love.

But when our Christmas is over, what shall we do with all that love? Pack it away with the rest of the trimmings? Or plant it and let it grow?

It's just a thought . . .

READING

Colossians 2:6-7

As you therefore have received Christ Jesus the Lord, continue to live your lives in him, rooted and built up in him and established in the faith, just as you were taught, abounding in thanksgiving.

PRAYER

Living God, we so soon get weary in doing good! Moved by your Spirit we love for a time. Then, satisfied that we have 'done our bit', we return to our old selfish ways. Help us to root our love in your goodness so that, like a live tree, it will continue to grow.

90

Surprise, surprise

Christmas used to be a time of surprises. Can you remember the excitement of a stocking full of small rustling parcels which defied definition until they were opened in the early hours? Nowadays we tend to ask people what they would like. Lists are produced, 'tokens' exchanged, or we say, 'Here is the money – you had better choose it yourself!'

Of course this way we avoid a lot of blunders. At least Dad doesn't have a drawer full of ties that he wouldn't be seen dead in! No longer does Laura have to put up with winter underwear four sizes too big when she was longing for a mini-bikini, and Aunt Jessica doesn't get lumbered with her thirty-ninth bottle of Eau de Cologne!

On the other hand, perhaps we have lost some of the magic of Christmas. The spontaneous joy of giving has become more of a mathematical exercise.

Most of us would admit to a secret love of surprises. The unexpected posy of flowers, the parcel with a blurred postmark, or the tiny gift on the tree which shows that someone has gone to the trouble of finding out what we really did want, give us more delight than the most elaborate present we have purchased and wrapped for ourselves.

God is very good at surprises. He is the Past Master of the unexpected. The beauty of a hyacinth which emerges from a dreary old bulb; the quivering perfection of a butterfly breaking free from an apparently dead chrysalis; the brilliance of a rainbow appearing in a rain-filled sky . . . the list is endless as we look at the world he has created.

And, at Christmas, came the greatest surprise of all . . . a Baby, born in a stable, who was to save the world.

It's just a thought . . .

READING

Luke 2:8-12

In that region there were shepherds living in the fields, keeping watch over their flock by night. Then an angel of the Lord stood before them, and the glory of the Lord shone around them, and they were terrified. But the angel said to them, 'Do not be afraid; for see – I am bringing you good news of great joy for all the people: to you is born this day in the city of David a Saviour, who is the Messiah, the Lord. This will be a sign for you: you will find a child wrapped in bands of cloth and lying in a manger.'

PRAYER

God of the unexpected, you never fail to surprise us. Your world is full of wonder and delight. The mystery of your love amazes us and takes us unawares. Give us the imagination to respond to your transforming grace.

91

Touchdown

Flying is a wonderful way to travel – above the traffic chaos, above the hurly-burly of suburbia, even above the clouds. But no matter how exhilarating the flight there is always the moment of relief when we 'touchdown' safely back to earth.

Touchdown is the moment when an aircraft comes into contact with the landing surface, but this in no way describes the sensation of returning to the environment we know, the things we understand. 'Fasten seatbelts and prepare to land' is a signal for a return to the familiar, and whether we have a smooth landing or come down to earth with a bump may depend on the preparations which have been made by the pilot and ground staff alike. The speed, the signals, the timing, the flare path or the people in the control tower prepare us for that moment of contact.

In a way, Christmas is the 'touchdown' of God. 'He came down to earth from heaven, who is God and Lord of all; and his shelter was a stable and his cradle was a stall.' The season of Advent reminds us of God's preparations: the prophets, the angels and John the Baptist all pointing the way. For our part December is fraught with plans: the shopping, baking, decorating; the carols, the cards, the crowds . . . our feet barely touch the ground. We are so busy getting ready for Christmas, we scarcely have time to get ready for Christ!

We need a little space for 'touchdown'. There in the stable a baby is born who will change the world. Amidst all the celebrations we could so easily miss the touch of his love.

It's just a thought . . .

READING

Isaiah 40:3-5

A voice cries out:
'In the wilderness prepare the way of the Lord,
make straight in the desert a highway for our God.
Every valley shall be lifted up, and every
mountain and hill be made low;
the uneven ground shall be made level,
and the rough places a plain.
Then the glory of the Lord shall be revealed,
and all the people shall see it together,
for the mouth of the Lord has spoken.'

PRAYER

Adventurous God, you risked everything to rescue our troubled world. Help us to make time and space to receive your precious gift of Jesus and to be ready for your touchdown in our lives.

92

Crackers!

It was suppertime and we all gathered round the table for our traditional evening meal – cold turkey and salad, trifle and cheese, with candles and crackers to round off the day.

Red and white, silver and green, with crisp crêpe fringes and gauzy bows, the crackers delighted our eyes. And on the box was the promise of pleasures to come: contents – hat, novelty and motto. In eager anticipation we crossed hands and pulled, and the party went with a bang! Then there was a great unravelling and reading of riddles and donning of paper crowns as we gleefully examined our 'prizes'.

Auntie E. at eighty-three was delighted with her plastic parachutist even though his descent was somewhat erratic. Uncle G. flirted with his paper fan and swapped it for Grandma's spinning top. We had penny whistles and parasols, Chinese puzzles and lucky charms. Secretly we all hoped for the coveted diamond ring! The excitement was intense until one of the children cried, 'There's nothing in mine!'

Unbelievable! Monstrous! It couldn't be! We searched among the debris of burnt-out bangers, paper and bows. The trimmings were there, but the contents were nil!

We all rallied round with sweets and consolations, offering our plastic Rolls Royce as compensation – but it was not the same. Nothing could atone for the let-down of that moment.

When Christmas is over, we venture into another year. Was our Christmas a 'cracker'? Beautifully decorated? Noisy?

Nostalgic? And were all the 'contents' there: the cheer, the compassion, the challenge of the Christ Child? For when the party is over we need something to take home and *God's* gift is for everyone and for all time to come.

It's just a thought . . .

READING

Isaiah 9:2a and 6

The people who walked in darkness
have seen a great light;
those who lived in a land of deep darkness –
on them light has shined.
For a child has been born for us,
a son given to us;
authority rests upon his shoulders;
and he is named
Wonderful Counsellor, Mighty God,
Everlasting Father, Prince of Peace.

PRAYER

God of celebration, you alone know the contents of our hearts. Look kindly on our festivities we pray, and when the party is over and we return to everyday, grant that we may not leave empty-handed but take with us the gift of your love for evermore.

93

Fools rush in

It was a cold winter morning a few years ago when I did just that! I was rushing around a shopping precinct in search of something special when I charged into a large store and nearly knocked myself out. I just could not believe it for a moment, for what I had taken to be an open doorway was in fact a large solid pane of glass! I must confess I was very shaken – not only by the tremendous blow to my nose which was cut and bruised (although the door remained intact) but also by the astonishing fact that I could have been so stupid.

We *do* rush in sometimes, believing that we know where we are going – jumping to conclusions, convinced that things are as *we* see them. And sometimes we come up against obstacles that we never even realised were there.

'Headstrong' would perhaps be better named 'headweak'! Maybe it would be best to stand back and take a good look before we hurl ourselves into action. Things are not always what they seem, as I painfully discovered. Now I always look twice for the doorway!

In the same way our relationships with others are sometimes hindered by invisible barriers. There are barriers of ignorance, mistrust and prejudice which come between people of different backgrounds, race or lifestyle, whether they be our next-door neighbours, our schoolfriends or the nations of the world.

It is not a bit of good our trying to walk through these plate glass windows, still less to believe they are not there. But what we can and must do is to open the door so that we may live in God's way, enabling understanding, enlightenment and tolerance to pass through.

It's just a thought . . .

READING

Hosea 14:9

Those who are wise understand those things;
    those who are discerning know them.
For the ways of the LORD are right,
    and the upright walk in them,
    but transgressors stumble in them.

PRAYER

Most wise and patient God, while we go rushing in, you stand at the door and knock. Give us the discerning love which treads gently in your footsteps. Save us from rash judgements and arrogant assumptions. Take us by the hand and lead us in your way.

94

The waiting game

There we were at the bus-stop on a damp winter morning. Umbrellas up, boots shuffling around on the gritty pavement, shopping bags and briefcases poised – all eyes on the horizon – waiting for a bus.

At first a few pleasantries were exchanged: 'Morning!' 'Cold again!' 'Been waiting long?' interspersed with some fidgeting of feet, tapping of watches and murmurs of discontent. The queue grew longer, the conversation more desultory as we debated the state of the nation, the National Health Service and the price of fish.

Suddenly there was an upsurge of excitement; at last the bus appeared. Umbrellas and pushchairs were folded, bags and babies hoisted on to shoulders – all set to go . . . then amidst signs of dismay the bus, with the legend 'Sorry – not in service' emblazoned across the front, drove straight past! 'What a waste of time,' said someone, 'We could have walked by now.'

We spend a great deal of our time waiting. Waiting in queues, in waiting rooms and traffic jams. Waiting to see the doctor, the dentist, the DSS! Waiting to buy stamps, to pay bills, to draw our money from the bank. What a waste of time . . !

A charming Indian lady who had spent long hours in hospital outpatients departments told me how she had come to terms with the waiting game.

'Why are you fretting?' she would ask her fidgety companions waiting for an ambulance to take them home. 'Is someone waiting for you? What will you do when you get home? Time is your own . . . Why don't you relax and make the most of it here? It's warm and bright, there is plenty to see and people to talk to. You will make yourselves ill with agitation when you could be benefiting from the rest!' This from a one-time dancer who was now confined to a wheelchair.

We are all waiting for something. Waiting for our holiday, for the weather to improve, waiting till we leave school or retire from work. Waiting till the children are out of nappies or until we move to a bigger house. Then, we feel, life will indeed begin. The truth is that life *has* begun – this is it – and every moment is precious in the sight of God. When it comes to living, why wait?

It's just a thought . . .

READING

Psalm 118:24

This is the day that the LORD has made;
    let us rejoice and be glad in it.

PRAYER

Eternal God, you are our 'Time-Lord'. While we wait impatiently for things to change, time is passing us by. We know that your timeless love surrounds us every moment of our lives. When we have time on our hands, help us to put it into your hands and so make every second count.

95

The hearth of the matter

How lovely it is to see a real log fire! I remember going to the Norfolk coast late in the year. The weather was cold and damp, and as darkness fell, a clammy sea mist enveloped us. We arrived at a small village guest house, chilled and somewhat disappointed with our glimpse of the grey North Sea. Then we were welcomed into the family lounge where a huge log fire was burning in the hearth, its leaping flames filling the friendly room with light and warmth. The surrounding brass ornaments glowed and twinkled and, as we toasted our frozen hands and feet at that hospitable fireside, it was impossible not to feel an inner glow of happiness.

Central heating has many advantages and it would be fanciful to yearn for the old days of smoky fuel and dirty grates, but there is within most of us a nostalgia for the family hearth which we gather around to relax and be comforted – not only in a practical way, but also in a spiritual way. Perhaps this is why we fit our gas and electric fires with make-believe logs and coal. Certainly there is a sensation of warmth which emanates from the glow of the firelight bulb even when the heating element is not switched on!

It seems that we need to *see* the fire in order to fully appreciate its warmth. No wonder the yule log is a symbol of Christmas.

I think that God knew this when he sent the baby Jesus into our dark world so that we could see and feel his love for us. And so it is with the world today – people need to see our love in action in order to warm their own hearts with its glow.

It's just a thought . . .

READING

James 2:14-17

What good is it, my brothers and sisters, if you say you have faith but do not have works? Can faith save you? If a brother or sister is naked and lacks daily food, and one of you says to them, 'Go in peace; keep warm and eat your fill', and yet you do not supply their bodily needs, what is the good of that? So faith by itself, if it has no works, is dead.

PRAYER

Loving God, you demonstrated your love for us by sending your Son to live amongst us. Help us to demonstrate our love for you by caring for one another.

96

Come inside!

When the cold winds of winter blow, icicles form, and the snow drifts up to our very doorsteps, our first reaction to anyone who calls is to bring them into the warmth with a friendly 'Come inside!'

The bitter weather sparks off a spirit of neighbourliness which a crisis always evokes – a chance for the community to show that it really does care. Perhaps then we make a special effort to remember the homeless and to set up shelters and provide hot soup. Perhaps then, if we are fortunate enough to have a warm and well-lit home, we feel we want to reach out and bring others inside.

However, I remember the house in Exeter where one of our daughters lived as a student. She told us it was so cold you could always see your breath indoors – even on a hot day – and wellington boots left in the hall overnight in winter were still covered in snow the next morning! Rumour had it that you put butter *in* the fridge to soften it. And you were glad to get out of doors in the mornings to warm up!

It is not always warmer *inside*! It takes more than central heating to thaw out a frosty atmosphere, and more than a gas fire to melt a cold heart. We need to be sure that those who venture over our threshold will be able to warm themselves in the glow of kindness and compassion. And if we hope to bring others in to share our Christian fellowship we must make sure that what we are offering is relevant to their needs. We need to be flexible enough to recognise that our 'set menu' may be too formal for those who are hungry for love, and our pews too hard for those who need a seat by the fire.

It's just a thought . . .

READING

Romans 12:9-13

Let love be genuine; hate what is evil, hold fast to what is good; love one another with mutual affection; outdo one another in showing honour. Do not lag in zeal, be ardent in spirit, serve the Lord. Rejoice in hope, be patient in suffering; persevere in prayer. Contribute to the needs of the saints; extend hospitality to strangers.

PRAYER

God of warmth and understanding, light a fire of love within our hearts, so that all for whom the world is cold and bleak may know that they are welcome at your fireside.

97

The inner glow

The fairy lights have been switched off, the candles blown out, the decorations taken down and, without ceremony, we are wrapped in the grey skies of winter once more. I'm not sure who did it or when it happened. There was much publicity about the switching *on* of the Christmas lights but not a lot said about the switching off. They just seemed to peter out.

Sadly the same thing sometimes seems to happen with our enthusiasm. After a great moment of uplift or 'conversion' when we want to tell the world about our experience, the excitement fades and the light diminishes in the day to day routine of life until the flame which burnt so brightly dies unnoticed.

Everyone seemed determined that we should have a bright Christmas this year! Among our presents was a battery-operated lantern for which many possible uses were suggested: going out into the shed at night; illuminating evening picnics at stately homes; walking down the railway line after a breakdown; or even for use in dimly-lit restaurants to help us see what we are eating!

But one of my favourite gifts was a little round candle which, the instructions read, 'will glow with a warm lantern effect when lit – the design illuminated by the radiant inner flame'.

When we encounter a dark spell in our lives no amount of exterior lighting will dispel the gloom. It is no use hanging up the fairy lights or decorations to relieve a sadness of the soul. It is then that we need an 'inner glow' to warm our hearts. A glow that comes from the assurance of God's love for us and shows us his design illuminated by the radiant inner flame.

It's just a thought . . .

READING

Isaiah 60:19-20

The sun shall no longer be your light by day, nor for brightness shall the moon give light to you by night; but the Lord will be your everlasting light, and your God will be your glory. Your sun shall no more go down, or your moon withdraw itself; for the Lord will be your everlasting light, and your days of mourning shall be ended.

PRAYER

Giver of light, glow within our hearts we pray, so that the radiance of your love may be reflected in our lives.

98

The big cover-up

It always comes as a surprise when winter arrives and we are unexpectedly wrapped in a blanket of snow! With exquisite precision, millions of tiny flakes, each unique in its perfect design, combine to transform our world into a work of art.

Each tiny leaf and twig is singled out for the artist's brush; bushes are adorned with bonnets of snow and icicles glitter in the occasional shaft of winter sunshine. Even mundane things like dustbins and clothes-lines assume a new dignity bedecked with their icing of pristine white, and the squalid junk along the railway sidings, the demolition sites and the council tip are hidden under a glistening veil – the great cover-up.

I suspect we have all done it at times: pushed the out-of-date newspapers under a cushion, kicked the discarded shoes under the sofa or bundled the ironing into a cupboard the moment before a visitor arrived! Even the nurses who delivered our last baby in something of a hurry were guilty of putting on their aprons *after* the event to impress the doctor when he came . . . the great cover-up.

I must confess to having sometimes urged my husband to do a quick painting job with 'just a dab of emulsion' but always in vain, for he invariably insists that any job worthwhile needs careful preparation – rubbing down, filling holes, and so on– in order to achieve a lasting result. No quick cover-up there!

And when the snow begins to melt under the tramp of a thousand muddy feet, and the slush turns black with the traffic's diesel fumes, and the ice breaks on the polluted river, we see that underneath the great cover-up nothing has changed.

Sometimes our spiritual life is like that too. Touched by a kindness from an unexpected source, or uplifted by a particularly moving service in church, we catch a vision of a world transformed. But if that transformation is to last we need to do more than paper over the cracks! It may mean much hard work and a serious rethink about what we are doing with our time and talents – a real 'snow-plough-and-shovel-job' to sort out the debris that underlies our human society and to make 'all things new'.

It's just a thought . . .

READING

Psalm 51:6-7, 10-11

You desire truth in the inward being;
therefore teach me wisdom in my secret heart.
Purge me with hyssop, and I shall be clean;
wash me, and I shall be whiter than snow.
Create in me a clean heart, O God,
and put a new and right spirit within me.
Do not cast me away from your presence,
and do not take your holy spirit from me.

PRAYER

Transforming God of love, come to our world we pray, not to cover up our deficiencies but to change the hearts of your people. Work within us so that we may not be tempted to gloss over the evil that is in the world, but to rebuild our society on the foundations of your truth.

99

Winter walk

Our five-year-old grandson told us that there are three rules for walking in the woods:

1. Keep your neck warm
2. Don't let the water come over your wellies, and
3. Look where you are going!

An experienced dog-walker, he is sometimes allowed to hold the lead when exercising Tumbo the deerhound who towers above him in amiable companionship as they follow the path between the trees. Do you remember those winter walks to and from school? Scuffing through the leaves, splashing in puddles, walking on walls, and trying not to tread on the lines between the paving stones; slipping and sliding on the icy patches or making footprints in untrodden snow. The world was our winter wonderland. Best of all was the jovial comradeship of our friends who trudged with us, exchanging confidences on the way and egging one another on to more and more daring deviations from the path!

Nowadays, for various reasons, children are often taken to school by car while we ourselves are transported from door to door on wheels! Our journey may be quicker and more comfortable, but it is only when we have experienced the elements, felt the wind on our faces or the snow on our boots that we can fully appreciate the delight of coming in to the warmth of home.

Our lives are often described as a walk – never as a car ride! As for the three rules, we could adapt them for our journey:

1. Wrap the comfort of God close about you
2. Don't let the troubles of the world overwhelm you, and
3. Keep your eyes on the one who knows the way.

It's just a thought . . .

READING

Proverbs 6:20-22 and 4:25-26

My child, keep your father's commandment,
and do not forsake your mother's teaching.
Bind them upon your heart always;
tie them around your neck.
When you walk, they will lead you;
when you lie down, they will watch over you;
and when you awake, they will talk with you.

Let your eyes look directly forward,
and your gaze be straight before you.
Keep straight the path of your feet, and all your ways will be sure.

PRAYER

God of the great outdoors, be with us as we walk in life's winter.
When the cold wind blows, envelop us in the warmth of your
love. When our feet slip, hold on to us and save us from falling,
and show us your light when we are not sure which way to go.

100

Who's counting?

So, you've had another birthday; another milestone has been passed. If it was your fourth you are probably proud to be starting school. If it was your eighteenth you may be recognised as an adult. If it was your fortieth you may just as soon not let on, and if it was your sixtieth you would probably prefer to be forty again! It's only when you reach your eighties that you really begin to boast about your age. Many of us do not care to advertise our birthdays simply because society has conditioned us to categorise people by age, and our expectations of worth and behaviour are coloured by a date on the calendar.

Now that we are hurtling towards the millennium there are many projects in hand to commemorate the passing of a thousand years. Shall we build a memorial, open a pleasure park, have a firework display or send up balloons? Whatever the plans, expectations are high that somehow the millennium will usher in a new age, and yet many will not stop to consider *why?*

It was about two thousand years ago that God sent his only Son into the world to demonstrate his love and to show us a new way to live. Whether we believe or not, it is significant that our system of dates is based on that event. It has taken a long time for God's message to get through, and our world is still full of strife. Surely the only true celebration of the millennium would be a fresh dedication of our lives to the creation of a society where there is justice and peace, and where the poor and underprivileged, the outcasts and the oppressed are enfolded in that love. As sunrise follows sunset, the ages roll on, and whether we enter the new century with expectation or trepidation, we can be sure that God goes with us. For in his eyes life is not measured by a counting of days and years, but by the height and depth of love.

Our God is the God of past, present and future and his promise and presence is with us for all eternity.

It's just a thought . . .

READING

Psalm 90:1-2 and 4

Lord, you have been our dwelling place
in all generations.
Before the mountains were brought forth,
or ever you had formed the earth and the world,
from everlasting to everlasting you are God.
For a thousand years in your sight
are like yesterday when it is past,
or like a watch in the night.

PRAYER

Eternal God, in whose hands are all the ages, lead us into a new era of faith. Help us to understand that days or years are both alike to you, and that all that counts is the measure of your love.